Heavenly Sex

Heavenly Sex

Sexuality in the Jewish Tradition

Dr. Ruth K. Westheimer
and Jonathan Mark

CONTINUUM • NEW YORK

1996

The Continuum Publishing Company
370 Lexington Avenue
New York, NY 10017

Printed in the United States of America

Library of Congress Cataloging-in-Publication Data
Westheimer, Ruth K. (Ruth Karola), 1928-
Heavenly sex : sexuality in the Jewish tradition / Dr. Ruth K.
Westheimer and Jonathan Mark.
p. cm.
ISBN 0-8264-0904-0 (alk. paper; pbk.)
1. Sex—Religious aspects—Judaism. 2. Judaism—Doctrines.
I. Mark, Jonathan. II. Title.
BM720.S4W47 1996
296.3'8566—dc20   95-4421
CIP

I would like to dedicate this book to the memory of my entire family who perished during the Holocaust, thankful that they had the opportunity of instilling in me the much cherished values of the Jewish tradition before they were lost to me. I am especially grateful to my father who "learned" with me, even though I was not a boy, and to my grandmother who, before her deportation, wrote in every letter to me that I should study and trust in God.

One of the pieces of Jewish lore that my father taught me was that Rabbi Mattithiah ben Heresh said: "vo-h'-vay Zanov La-arayot V'al T'hee Rosh La-Shu-a-leem—Be a tail to lions and not a head to foxes" (Pirke Avot 4:20).

This wise teaching tells us that we cannot be experts on everything, but that our contributions can be an adornment to even the most learned or the most powerful. It is another way of expressing the rabbinic Midrash that teaches that we learn from the giants who precede us, but by standing on the shoulders of their accomplishments we can see even beyond their vision and chart new directions.

I also dedicate this book to my family of now: my husband, Fred; our daughter, Miriam Westheimer, Ed.D., and her husband, Joel Einleger; and, with his most recent academic achievement, our son, Joel

Westheimer, Ph.D.; and especially to my grandson, Ari.

—Ruth K. Westheimer

This book is dedicated to Ruchy.

—Jonathan Mark

Contents

Acknowledgments

I would like to thank the following people who have continued with their support and friendship over all of these years: Mary Cuadrado, Rabbi and Mrs. Leonard Kravitz, Rabbi William Lebeau, Rabbi and Mrs. Robert Lehman, Rabbi and Mrs. Schlomo Riskin, Rabbi Selig Salkowitz, Josh Gafni, Ellen Goldberg, Alfred Kaplan, Marga and Bill Kunreuther, Pierre and Joanne Lehu, Lou Lieberman, Ph.D., Werner Linz, John and Ginger Lollos, Dale Ordes, Fred and Ann Rosenberg, Cliff Rubin, Rose and Simeon Schreiber, Amir Shaviv, Geoffrey Wigoder, Ben Yagoda, and special thanks to my friends at New York University Press including Colin Jones, director of NYU Press, Niko Pfund, our superb editor in chief, and Despina Papazoglou Gimbel, our managing editor.

—Ruth K. Westheimer

I must first acknowledge the glory of God, who created male and female, sex and love for heavenly purpose. Whatever in this volume is not pleasing to the reader, the fault lies with the humble authors and not with the Holy One or the traditions of His people.

This book is also dedicated to and inspired by my wife, Ruth, God's gift to me, whose continuous love, encouragement, good humor, wisdom, insight, and support made this project possible, along with our children, Sara Noa Nechama and Rebecca Yona Moriah.

I have the greatest appreciation for the friendship of Allan Leicht and Renee, who introduced Dr. Westheimer to me, among their many gifts. Gratitude is also due to my parents, Elaine and Mordecai Lippa ben-Yitzhak Zev, may his memory be a blessing; to my ancestors, back through the centuries, who kept the traditions alive; to Deborah Mark, Naomi and Rabbi Tsvi Blanchard, and Stephen Kaufman, for their unique generosity and encouragement; Rabbi Shlomo Carlebach whose romance with Torah remains an inspiration; Rabbi Meir Fund for his dreams and teachings about dreams; to all the great rebbes of Breslov, Pishishka, Lubavitch, Lizinsk, and Izbiche; to Eric Nooter; and to colleagues and friends at the *Jewish Week* and throughout Jewish journalism.

Thanks again to our editors at NYU Press, and to those who shared with us their heavenly secrets, fears, fantasies, and romantic adventures.

—Jonathan Mark

One

Peace in the Home

L ong before I became "Dr. Ruth," when I was still a good little girl named Karola Ruth Siegel growing up in an Orthodox Jewish home in Frankfurt am Main, Germany, I wasn't used to saying or hearing words such as penis, vagina, orgasm, or clitoris. If, through some fluke, I did hear such words, I'd find myself blushing.

Sometimes I still blush. We were European Jews, more European than Jewish, and thoroughly influenced by the prudish Victorian attitudes of that era—attitudes still influencing the way so many of us think, act, and talk about sex. Why, when talking about sex, do I need to add that we were more European than Jewish? Simply because if our attitudes were more Jewish than European, we would have been more open and adventurous about sex than most people think possible, including many Jews who are unfamiliar with their own tradition.

What did the Victorian mother tell her daughter on the night of her wedding? "Grit your teeth and think of England." But in the Jewish tradition, there are hints, incentives, and even legislation for orgasms—yes, a woman's, too.

Especially a woman's. In the Jewish marriage ceremony, sexual satisfaction is part of the contract. Under the wedding canopy, a groom promises his bride that he will provide her with comfortable standards of food, shelter, and sexual gratification. The holiest men are required to marry. Celibacy is not a virtue—orgasms are.

Some ancient rabbis advise that if a man brings his wife to orgasm before he ejaculates he will be rewarded with a son—a reward thought to be as precious to the man as an orgasm is satisfying to a woman. As a sexologist I know how important it is that a woman not engage in sexual activity continually without having an orgasm. And here there is even a spiritual tradition that clearly understands that in a sexual relationship both partners must be sensitive to the sexual needs of the other. Of course, the equation of orgasmic satisfaction and the gender of a child seems harsh to the modern observer, as well it should. Nevertheless, it is a marvel that the sages back in antiquity were so concerned with encouraging and educating their followers to the notion that a woman's orgasm exists, is precious, and that a woman does not simply exist as a subordinate vessel for the man.

The Jewish writer Maurice Samuel jokes that "Jews are too busy having children to bother with sex," but the tradition in fact encourages a husband and wife to have sex not just for procreation, but for pleasure. In the synagogue libraries and study halls of Frankfurt, they studied a rabbinic commentator known as the Ramban (the popular acronym of Rabbi Moshe Ben-Nachman, Nachmanides), considered among the greatest rabbis of the millennia. Though he lived from 1195 to 1270, he was spoken of and quoted in the present tense, as if he were still alive. He taught that a husband may act with his wife "in any manner whatsoever, and kiss any organ of her body he wishes, and have intercourse naturally or unnaturally." He advises couples to use different positions while making love, including entry of the woman's vagina from behind (interesting from a sex thera-pist's point of view, since the exposed clitoris provides possi-bilities for greater pleasure).

Sex is not only for reproduction but for recreation. But how does a couple, raised with the traditional values that promote sexual modesty, obtain the sexual confidence to try different sexual positions and express sexual needs? How do you teach young, modest men and women to take their clothes off and give and take pleasure, to touch and love in ways that are not "standard"? Maybe this is one of the reasons the tradition urges people at the flowering of their sexual energy and desire to spend less time on sublimation and more on the enjoyment of sex as a mitzvah—a Divine command.

One *rebbetzin* (as the wife of a rabbi is called), for in-stance, teaches a bridal class to women who are soon to be married. The rebbetzin advises the brides that "chicken soup all the time is not very interesting." Nor is the same sexual diet. If this is not the sort of instruction we expect from the wife of a rabbi, the fault lies with us, for what the rebbetzin teaches is totally in keeping with this very sexy, very unpubli-cized tradition.

Judaism is intensely sexual. Ramban taught in his *Igeret HaKodesh:* "When sexual intercourse is done for the sake of Heaven, there is nothing so holy and pure. . . . God did not create anything that is ugly or shameful. If the sexual organs are said to be shameful, how can it be said that the Creator fashioned something blemished?" Adds the *Zohar,* the most important of Jewish mystical texts: "The Divine Presence rests on the marital bed when both male and female are united in love and holiness. Where there is no union of male and female, people are not worthy of beholding the Divine

Presence. . . . After the destruction of the Jerusalem Temple, the bedroom in each home was considered as an aspect of the once glorious and sanctified Holy of Holies."

The great rabbi, Simeon ben-Halafta, called the penis "the great peacemaker of the home," an interesting choice of words since the Hebrew translation for "peace in the home," *shalom bayit,* is the Jewish blessing given to every couple, and prayed for by everyone. Maybe I didn't hear the words "penis" and "vagina" when I was growing up, but come to think of it, I did hear a lot of prayers for shalom bayit.

These concepts allow us to teach men and women that peace in the home is inseparable from good sex. They empower unsatisfied partners by suggesting that, if a problem exists, they must take the responsibility to get aroused, and teach each other how they need to be satisfied, how to be touched, how much pressure, how much foreplay. A partner cannot guess these things, no matter how much he or she loves the spouse.

Good sex is inseparable from good communication, which is sensitive and kind communication. Today we teach women to be assertive. But if a woman says to her partner, "Either you get it up or I'm leaving," he is not going to have an erection and she will be left as disappointed as Madame Potiphar, to whom we will return in chapter 2.

The Biblical word that is used to inform us that our Biblical heroes had sex is *la'da'at,* "to know." To know someone sexually is to know that the sexual experience is much more than just a penis inside a vagina. Sex is a touch, a smile, communication: the way we know each other, the way we move, the way we express ourselves. In the Jewish tradition a husband must talk sweetly to his wife when initiating intercourse; this has a psychological as well as a physiological basis.

But how is a young religious couple, presumably modest and relatively inexperienced, "to know" how to go about having good sex? There's a story in the Talmud about a rabbi (known simply as Rav) who was having sex with his wife on Friday night, after a very good Shabbos meal. (There is actually a commandment that a rabbi must have sex with his wife at least once a week, preferably on Friday night.) Well, the rabbi was really enjoying himself, and we assume his wife was too, though the Talmud does not tell us. Yet while the rabbi was doing all of the things that once made me blush, he suddenly had a strange feeling that there was a third person in the room. He got up, looked behind the curtain, looked in the closet, looked under the bed, and lo and behold there was his favorite student (Rabbi Kahana) hiding under the bedsprings.

Rav said: "Is this *derech eretz,* is this proper behavior for a yeshiva boy to be under the rabbi's bed while the rabbi performs the *mitzvah* [God's commandment] of intercourse?"

The yeshiva boy answered: "Rabbi, what you are doing is a mitzvah from the Torah, and I must learn from you!"

What is interesting here is Judaism's braiding of sexual openness and sexual modesty. The yeshiva boy convinces the rabbi that his audacity is legitimate because knowing how to perform intercourse is a legitimate part of his religious and spiritual education. Nevertheless, the boy understands that he must hide. This dialectic is ongoing, not only within the tradition but within each of us who seeks to balance our need for modesty and privacy with our need for sexual education.

Judaism is a messianic religion, but there is no messianism without men and women coming together. In the Babylonian Talmud's tractate Brachot, signs are revealed to recognize the end of the premessianic "exile." The Talmud says: "The night [symbolic of the exile] is divided into three phases. In the first, donkeys are braying. In the second, dogs are barking. In the final phase, mothers nurse their babies and lovers talk in whispers."

As the Sabbath is the simulation of a messianic world, celebrated by married couples making love, so the dawning of messianism is marked by a successful family in which parents relate to each other and to their children with nurturing and love.

As Rabbi Shlomo Carlebach says, "People say they don't know how to pray, they don't know how to talk to God. But if you know how to talk to your wife or your husband, if you know how to talk to your children, you can talk to the Holy One as easily."

Ritual as routine is a disaster. Ritual, however, can be transformed into a poetic expression of our sexual and better selves.

When I started my clinical work, I was a real greenhorn. One day, as I was assisting a psychiatrist at the clinic, in walks an Orthodox woman, terribly shy. Looking out from under the *tichel* kerchief that covered her hair, she told us that she has never had an orgasm. We all know it's not easy to talk about sexual function, so this was not an easy thing to say. Women think that men talk so openly about sex. Well, they may talk openly when they are bragging, but it is very rare for a man to tell another man, "Last night I couldn't get an erection."

The psychiatrist proceeded to take a typical psychiatric

and medical history. One of his questions was, "Do you ever have intercourse during menstruation?" Thereupon the young lady got up and walked out. At the time I was too inexperienced to tell the doctor the error of his ways. Coming from an Orthodox home, I knew that asking an Orthodox woman a question involving the laws of sexual purity and abstinence during menstruation would be so threatening to her that we might never see her again.

She indeed may have felt some sexual arousal during menstruation, as some women do, and she may have felt guilty about it, knowing the Orthodox taboo against sex during menstruation—a taboo that extends another five days following the last sight of blood.

That day I made the decision that one of my professional responsibilities would be to work with Jewish men and women who want "peace in the home," and don't quite know how to get it.

It has always been easier for me to be explicit, and to help religious patients be explicit, precisely because I am a traditional Jew, and traditional Jews ought to have no reason to be shy when discussing sex. After all, we don't know much about God other than what He has given us in the Bible. Genesis, the first book of the Bible, contains only a handful of laws, but one of the first is to make love and have many children: "A man should leave his mother and father and cleave unto his wife. . . . Be fruitful and multiply."

The Bible is quite direct about sex, about the relationships of Biblical characters. Indeed, the early rabbis were equally honest about themselves. One of the Talmudic sages, Rabbi Meir, had a wife named Bruria, who is quoted several times in the Talmud—an example of influence that was quite rare for women of that generation or any other generation. One day, says Rashi in his commentary on the Talmud, Bruria criticized her husband's colleagues for calling women immature and irresponsible. Her husband was moved—perhaps pressured by his fellow sages—to test Bruria's own maturity and responsibility.

His choice of test may have revealed more about him than it did about her. He arranged for one of his yeshiva students to try to test her fidelity to both Reb Meir and God's law. Over time, after an extended seduction, the student and Bruria did indeed have intercourse. But then she killed herself in shame. This is an amazing legend. To those unfamiliar with the Jewish tradition, it may be even more amazing that the sages saw fit to print it—right alongside the main text in every edition of the Talmud.

Another story. Abbaye, one of the Talmud's most revered sages, tells about the time he overheard a man and a woman agree to travel together. "I will follow them," Abbaye said to himself, "and keep them from sinning." So he followed the attractive couple down the road, past the edge of town, past the fields, and on to a fork in the road. There he heard the man say to the woman as they parted, "Your company was lovely, and now the way is long." Abbaye returned to town and told his Talmudic colleagues, "If I were that man, I would not have been able to control myself." Imagine any of our religious leaders today being so honest, or a society where such honesty goes unpunished.

Although modesty and restraint are themes that abound in Judaism, there are also designated times and holidays when it is a particular command to bring single men and women together. In fact, one of these holidays—the midsummer Tu B'Av—is comparable to Yom Kippur in its festivity, according to the Talmud. The sages considered Yom Kippur a

festive day because on that day all were forgiven and returned to a state of grace—a gift of starting over that each
romance also seems to bring.

Holidays such as Tu B'Av (the name simply means the
fifteenth day of the Hebrew month of Av) give continuous
hope to those who are not married or in love. The cyclical
nature of the traditional Jewish calendar is a reminder that
there is always another season, another holiday, when it is a
blessing for women, all dressed in white, to go out and
dance, a time when women are given license to be seductive.
Although single women are taught to be modest, Jewish
tradition acknowledges that a man is more likely to be
aroused if a woman is somewhat seductive. The tradition
had to offer a counterpoint to modesty to allow this.

Aside from the festivities of Tu B'Av, there are also the
enduring images of Moses' sister Miriam and the women at
the Red Sea's crossing, playing their tambourines with all the
movements of erotic dance. What better foreplay than to see
women dancing? The women were never told just to sit
around and watch the men. The women were clearly told:
you dance separately, but you dance. Even the most modest
of yeshiva boys would throw a quick peek, a *coup d'oeil,* a
furtive, fast glance. And no one can tell a sex therapist like
me that a *coup d'oeil* at the right person is not sexually
arousing.

Sex, in and of itself, has never been a sin for Jews, or
something not to discuss. Within Sinai's covenantal boundaries, it is a mitzvah, a religious commandment. And what is
a mitzvah except a blessing, or a guide on how our lives can
be more heavenly? The Biblical injunction to have children
cannot be fulfilled if a man does not have an erection, or a
woman has no desire and refuses his advances. So the Jewish

tradition states that we must understand the mysteries of sexuality to understand the beauty and mysteries of God's law.

In the Jewish tradition, sex is very much in the mind of the beholder, in the mind where a healthy approach to sex made good sex possible for Jews in the most trying of circumstances and situations. As the Talmud teaches us in tractate Sanhedrin: If a man and a woman are truly lovers they can make their bed on the edge of a sword; if their love goes bad, the best bed in the world is not big enough.

Two

Beauty and the Bible

And they knew that they were naked

There is a Bible in every hotel and motel in the country, and quite rightly—the Bible is the oldest but still the wisest guide to sex ever written. People pick up the Bible for many different reasons but rarely, if ever, as a sex manual. That is their mistake.

We are not talking about a Bible that most people who have not read it associate with puritan chastity, but about the Jewish Bible, with its galaxies of commentaries in which sex is not only allowed but ordained. The Bible teaches that God created the world by separation—heaven from earth, light from dark, water from land, and mortality from immortality. The bridge between heaven and earth is sex, where the greatest pleasure known to humans is matched by the possibility of life being created from sexual union.

Part and parcel of the creation of sex is the creation of the concept of arousal—and make no mistake about it, say the sages, this was all designed by the Creator.

The rabbis were not shy about telling us that some of the most arousing women the world has ever known appear in the Bible. In the Babylonian Talmud, known as the Oral Law and said by tradition to have been given to Moses on Mount Sinai alongside the written Torah, we are told that there were four women of exceptional beauty in the world: Sara the matriarch; Abigail, wife of King David; Rahav, the Jericho madam who sheltered the Israelite spies and later married Joshua; and Queen Esther, of the Purim story told in her eponymous scroll.

In that same Talmudic passage, the rabbis taught that "Rahav inspired lust" by simply mentioning her name; Yael, an Israelite heroine from the Book of Judges, inspired lust with her voice; "Abigail, by remembering her"; and Michal, daughter of King Saul, "with her appearance." The Talmud doesn't stop there. Rabbi Yitzhak said, "Whoever says 'Rahav, Rahav,' will immediately have a seminal emission." But Rav Nachman said to his colleague "I say 'Rahav, Rahav,' and I am not concerned that anything might happen." To which Rabbi Yitzhak replied, "What I said was concerning a man who knows her and is familiar with her."

Male beauty was no less openly discussed. The Babylonian Talmud (Baba Mezia) offers the following discussion about Rabbi Yohanan, editor of the Jerusalem Talmud. Rabbi Yohanan claimed, "I am the only one remaining of Jerusalem's men of outstanding beauty." It is said that he used to go and sit at the gates of the *mikvah* ritualarium. When the daughters of Israel ascended from the bath, he would say, "Let them look at me, that they may bear sons as beautiful and as learned as I." The rabbis said to him, "Aren't you afraid of bringing an evil eye?" "I am descended from Joseph," he answered, "against whom an evil eye is powerless," as proven by the Biblical Joseph's ability to resist Madame Potiphar, as we will see later.

Resh Lakish, one of Rabbi Yohanan's contemporaries, was a tough character who associated with thieves and was rumored to have once been a thief himself. Once he was walking along the Jordan River when he saw a beautiful form bathing in the mist. Resh Lakish stripped and swam to it, but it was Rabbi Yohanan. Resh Lakish said to him, "Your beauty should belong to a woman," and Rabbi Yohanan replied, "Your strength should be for Torah."

Sex was something easily discussed, and even prostitution was not as scandalous as it is now. In the Talmud (Baba Mezia), the story is told of one rabbi who visited the town of Rabbi Eliezer, the son of Rabbi Simon. "Did that righteous man leave a son?" the rabbi asked. "Yes," he was told. "All the prostitutes who charge everyone two (zuzim coins) — they *pay him* eight!"

In the tractate Baba Basra, it is written that Eve, the first woman, was the most beautiful of all. But a debate rages about whether she, who was made from Adam's rib, can be compared to women born of earthly mothers.

Yes, in the beginning was the word, and the word was sex. From the first chapters of the Book of Genesis, God's introduction to humanity, it is apparent that here is a theology spanning from the dawn of history that accounts for psychology, sexology, and human passion. The Bible, the story of how men and women first came to know God, and the Talmud, the canonized commentary on the Bible, is also the story of how men and women came to know each other.

To God, the Holy Author of Genesis, where people went to bed was as important as where they went to pray. No sooner does the Good Book get underway than God says: "It is not good for man to be alone. . . . And the Lord God caused a deep sleep to fall over Adam, and he slept, and He took one of his ribs, and closed up the flesh in its place. And Adam said, 'This is now bone of my bone, flesh of my flesh. She shall be called Woman because she was taken out of man.' "

In the Talmud (Shabbat), Rabbi Kahana asked, "What is meant by the passage in Psalms 33:9, 'For he spoke and it came into being,'? This refers to a wife," that is, to Eve.

And why was she fashioned from a rib? Because, says the Midrash, it is the most chaste part of the body, not associated with any illicit, inappropriate inclinations or character traits that might be linked to other limbs and organs.

But she, too, was human. Before long the woman Eve was seduced by the serpent to eat from the forbidden tree in the midst of the garden. Eve ate from the tree, gave the fruit to Adam, and "then the eyes of both of them were opened and they knew that they were naked; they sewed fig leaves together and made themselves coverings." Elie Wiesel writes, "Without Eve, Adam would have been a man but not human."

And God told the woman, "I will greatly multiply your sorrow and your conception; in pain shall you bring forth children; your desire shall be for your husband, and he shall rule over you."

The tree's full and proper name was the Tree of Knowledge of Good and Evil, and most of the next fifty chapters of Genesis are devoted to the exploration of the potential of good and evil inherent in human relationships. In fact, throughout Genesis we are introduced to one saintly figure after another and are told almost nothing about them but their "nakedness," their pained relationships, and moments of sexual truth. With every passing Biblical generation, the characters become more and more daring and expressive regarding love or its absence.

Soon, however, God sent the Great Flood to destroy the world because "all flesh has corrupted his way upon the earth." The Talmud's Rabbi Yohanan says in tractate Sanhedrin that the sin of the generation of the Flood was that "cattle, beasts and men had intercourse with each other." The importance of sexuality is such that the Talmud emphasizes that the corruption was primarily sexual, rather than the corruption of social or religious misdemeanors. According to the tradition, there is almost no limit to sexual pleasure within marriage—even polygamous marriage in those days. But the world, said God, though sanctified by marriage contracts, is worthy of destruction when there is a hemorrhaging of sexual boundaries and the line between gender and species is erased beyond recognition, such as through homosexuality or even bestiality. The thought, in the ancient world, was that all living things are of equal holiness and worth, and why should there be a limit on sexual pleasure if a man can be pleased, say, by a sheep? It is worthwhile to note that in the Garden of Eden, humans were instructed only to eat vegetation. It was only after the Great Flood that God instructs man that animals could be consumed, and a demarcation between the species came into existence.

In other words, for want of a good sex therapist, the world was destroyed. And that is not meant to be flip. Every day on our nightly news and in our morning newspapers we learn how crimes of passion and sexual confusion continue to destroy thousands of individual "worlds" four thousand years after the Great Flood. Indeed, more than a millennium later, sexual immorality—particularly adultery—was again cited by the Talmud (Yoma) as one of the three reasons, on a par with a profusion of murder and idolatry, that caused the First Jerusalem Temple to be destroyed, a cataclysmic event still mourned by Jews today.

After the waters receded and Noah's children repopulated

the earth, the Bible introduces us to the matriarchs and patriarchs of the Israelite family—Abraham and Sara, Isaac and Rebecca, and Jacob, Rachel, and Leah—that are to be the prime characters in Genesis. Fittingly, the sign of the covenant between God and Abraham was to be on the penis, with God demanding the circumcision of Abraham and his male descendants for eternity. There was to be no sex without the sense of God, to sanctify the good and create the fear of God with the idea of luring Abraham and his descendants away from sexual crimes and misdemeanors.

Reb Nachman of Breslov, a famed nineteenth-century Hasidic master, taught in his book *Likutey Moharan* that circumcision involves two distinct acts. In the first, the *orlah,* the flesh covering the crown of the penis is removed. Afterward, the *krum,* the membrane beneath the skin, is peeled back until the flesh of the crown is visible. Reb Nachman explains that the orlah symbolizes evil that must be completely rejected. The krum is seen as the intermediary between the orlah and the flesh, indicating the good that is at times blended with the bad. The peeling of the krum symbolizes how good must be separated from evil. Indeed, the sexual urge and act are capable of the highest majesty—the creation of life. The very same penis and the very same act are capable of inducing a chain reaction of pain leading to death. It is this dialectic that drives the story of Judaism's attitudes toward sex.

No sooner do we meet Abraham and Sara than the Bible focuses on an unexpected conversation. Abraham says to his wife: "I realize that you are a beautiful woman. When the Egyptians see you, they will assume that you are my wife and kill me. . . . Please say that you are my sister. Then they will be good to me for your sake."

This is a rather remarkably blunt introduction to what is literally the "first family" of religion, yet it is what God tells us about the paradigmatic family of the Bible. A virtually identical story is told about Isaac and Rebecca, in which he asks her to pretend to be his sister so as to elude a king perceived by Isaac to be dangerous.

The sages see a moral in all this. Before a man and woman embark on the great adventure of having a relationship, they retain all their options and an abundance of choice. But as the relationship matures and deepens, as it would in marriage, options are voluntarily withdrawn and the couple graduates from "choice" to "no choice."

Secular culture suggests to us that choice is the better option. But let us think again. A parent to a child, a brother to a sister, are not relationships of choice. Yet they are the relationships that are the most likely to be of a lifetime's duration, through good times and bad. They are the relationships which theoretically produce the greatest responsibility. A brother and sister do not "break up" with each other, except in the most tragic and extraordinary situations.

And so, the rabbis say, when a man and a woman go into "Egypt," symbolic of the secular and sensual "outside world," the couple must care for each other on a deeper level. A mature man has "no choice" but to be responsible for his lover's emotional well-being, and responsible for the child that may come from their union. A mature lover has "no choice" but to be honest, committed, and to care for the other.

Abraham is essentially saying, "When we go into the world and are confronted by temptation, decadence, and seduction, let you and I pledge to each other and God that our relationship is more precious than that." He is proposing that marriage, ideally, is the process of taking two lovers and fusing them into immediate family.

It is also interesting to note that within this first-known marriage based on love and commitment, not only does the bride change her name—from Sarai to Sara—but Abraham does, too—from Abram to Abraham. They did so at God's command, indicative that their commitment to the Divine involved a rebirth.

And what of Adam and Eve's courtship and relationship? It was a relationship based less on love than on loneliness. At the first sign of trouble—when God asks Adam about eating the forbidden fruit—he immediately blames Eve, as if her fate were not his own. Such a relationship is doomed, fated for expulsion from Paradise. A relationship like Abraham and Sara's, however, where destiny is intertwined, is bound for the Promised Land.

Abraham and Sara also were the first couple to explode the myth that sex is just something for the young. "Now Abraham and Sara were old and advanced in years, and Sara had passed the age of childbearing," says the Bible. "Therefore Sara laughed within herself, saying, 'After I have grown old, shall I have pleasure, my lord [Abraham] of being old also?' "

But the Bible teaches that angels visited their tent and Sara had a child, Isaac, long after others thought it possible. Can angels visit any tent regardless of the age of its inhabitants, bringing sexual pleasure onto old age? The answer is found in the name she gave her child, Isaac, which means laughter. As Sara says, "God has made me laugh so that all who hear [this story] will laugh with me."

Sexual delight is often accompanied by good humor. Among the many messages that Sara may have wished to send to her millions of descendants was this: Enjoy laughter with your lover and you too will feel that angels are visiting your nighttime tent, bringing pleasure "onto our old age."

A similar story is told in the Second Book of Kings, when, centuries later, one of Sara's descendants, the prophet Elisha, promised a doubting woman that she, like Sara, would conceive despite the old age of her husband, and she did. In the Bible, not only did older people have sex, they were given successful blessings for conception as well.

It was not always easy on the individuals involved. In the Talmud (Yebamos), Rabbi Isaac said, "Our patriarch Isaac was impotent . . . as was Rebecca infertile (before Jacob and Esau were born). . . . Why were our ancestors childless (for so long)? Because the Holy One desires the prayers of the righteous."

Some stories in the tradition regarding the ability of the old or infirm to have a child are rather fanciful. The Talmud (Shabbat) relates that "it happened once that a man's wife died, leaving him a baby boy who was still nursing. The man was so poor that he could not pay a nursemaid. A miracle happened that the man's breast spread open like that of a woman's and he nursed his baby." In any case, it reveals the extent to which the tradition is willing to go in suggesting miracles for the possibilities of procreation and assisting the family once a child arrives.

However, the sages made it clear that, magical stories aside, those who are burdened by the frailties of aging and the inability to have children should not take it as a reflection of God's anger. The Talmud (Moed Katan) states that "longevity and fertility are based less on virtue than on genetics. This is illustrated by the case of Rabah and Rav Chisda, both of whom were great and holy men, so much so that either of them could bring down rain with their prayers. But Rav Chisda died at ninety-two; Rabah at forty. In the house of Rav Chisda were sixty marriages; by Rabah there were sixty deaths. And yet both sages were exalted, differentiated by genetics rather than merit.

Sex is a pleasure but not always a cure. Abraham's nephew Lot went to live in Sodom, a city infamous for its selfishness and synonymous forever after with immorality. Regarding Sodom, the Talmud's Rabbi Juda says in tractate Sanhedrin, "They were wicked with their bodies, and sinners with their money." But Abraham's holy family did not find it necessary to live in a monastery or demand that their neighbors be as saintly as they were. Sodom, though, did push the limits of just how bad a neighborhood could be.

When God told his friend Abraham that fire and brimstone would be poured upon Sodom, wiping it from the face of the earth, Abraham did not rejoice at the misfortune of sinners. Instead, he begged and bargained with God that the city be saved if there could be found only fifty, thirty, even ten Sodomites worth saving.

There were not, but Abraham did win the concession from God, who said, "If I find in Sodom ten righteous within the city then I shall spare all the place for their sakes."

What a different world the Jewish tradition promises here. Religious leaders, as epitomized by Abraham, would not threaten, demean, or point fingers at even the worst of their fellow men and women. From Abraham through the hasidic masters such as Reb Levi of Berditchiv, the masters of this tradition enlisted their "closeness" with God to act as defense attorneys for their less-than-holy brothers and sisters, rather than taking on the prosecuting role that too many modern religious leaders seem to embrace.

God's angels helped Lot and his family escape the destruction of Sodom (although Lot's wife was turned into a pillar of salt for looking back at the apocalyptic incineration). Lot and his two daughters found refuge in a cave. It seemed that the whole earth was engulfed in the apocalypse that destroyed Sodom.

Then the firstborn of Lot's daughters said to the younger, "There is no man on earth to come in to us as is the custom of all the earth. Come, let us make our father drink wine and we will sleep with him," so that the human race may live on. From this drunken incestuous night, a boy named Moab was born. Generations later, from Moab was born Ruth, the grandmother of King David and therefore the great-grandmother of the Messiah who is traditionally linked to the House of David. An ironic development from immorality, but we shall see in a later chapter the eschatological (messianic) reasoning.

Actually, the Talmud (Yebamos) states that "for the crime of incest one is able to offer repentance, but for the crime of fraudulent measures one cannot repent," because for the latter crime the offender does not know whom he cheated and cannot arrange for compensation or ask forgiveness.

If Lot's daughter is the "maternal side" of the Messiah's ancestry, Patriarch Jacob is the "paternal side." Unlike his grandfather Abraham, for whom Sara was the only one of his many wives that mattered to his personal and spiritual history, and unlike his father Isaac who was married only to Rebecca, Jacob had four wives—and simultaneously at that: the sisters Leah and Rachel, and his concubines Bilha and Zilpa. And Jacob not only got along with each of them, but we are told that he consulted them for general advice.

Jacob seemed as much involved with all his wives as another prominent bigamist in Genesis, Lemach. When Lemach, said to be the grandfather "of all who handle the lyre and the flute," was troubled after killing a man in self-defense, he cried out to both his wives, Ada and Zilla, rather than one wife or the other. Similar was the status of the many Mrs. Jacobs.

Wives and sensuality weren't much on Jacob's mind when he was a young student in the "smart class" at the yeshiva of Shem and Ever. But then he purchased his brother Esau's birthright for a bowl of lentil soup. The blessing that came with the birthright was the real prize. Jacob's father Isaac, old and blind, remarked to his disguised son: "Your voice is the voice of Jacob and your hands the hands of Esau." Some consider this sentence a simple statement of fact: the blind Isaac was caressing Jacob, who had his arms covered with animal skins, similar to his hairy brother Esau.

We, though, may interpret Isaac's words as yet another blessing Isaac could bestow upon his son: Isaac was telling Jacob that he should have the "arms," symbolizing the physical sensuality of Esau, while maintaining the poetic nature and seductive charms indicative of the "voice of Jacob."

Jacob's two most famous sons are Joseph and Judah. Virtually all Jews are said to be descended from Judah alone—the very name "Jew" is a derivative of Judah. Yet his story is one of sexual frustration, oddly unsettling for a man of Judah's stature but in keeping with Biblical themes.

Judah had a son named Er, who married a woman named Tamar. Sadly, Er died young and Judah told his other son, Onan, to fulfill the legal obligation of a dead man's brother by marrying the widow, for such was the law of the land when a brother died childless.

"Marry Tamar," said Judah to Onan. "You will then raise children to keep your brother's name alive."

Onan came into Tamar's tent that evening, but instead of impregnating her he spilled his seed on the ground—the original act of onanism. Whether he was a victim of premature ejaculation, whether he masturbated, or whether he intentionally withdrew is a matter of speculation. But God was less forgiving than a sex therapist, and Onan immediately joined Er in the other world.

Judah then said to Tamar, "I have one more son, Shelah, but he is young and I don't want him to die like my other two. Please wait until he is older before you spend the night with him, at which time he may fulfill his brotherly obligation."

Tamar was getting older and did not plan on being sexually deprived, or childless, in the prime of her life. Er and Onan's brother Shelah had grown to manhood and yet Shelah had not been given to Tamar as a husband. After years of deprivation, she heard that her recently widowed father-in-law, Judah, was going to the far-off town of Timna on sheep-shearing business. He was also seeking "consolation," says the Bible, after the death of his wife.

Tamar followed, put on a veil, sat by the place called Twin Wells where the prostitutes solicited, and was approached by none other than Judah, who did not recognize her through the veil that never left her face. Taking Judah's seal, cloak, and staff as her payment, the disguised Tamar made love to her father-in-law, and became pregnant from him. He never knew it was Tamar.

The two returned home separately, but people soon began whispering about the unwed Tamar's pregnancy. "Your daughter-in-law must have been running around with all the wrong people in all the wrong places," the princely Judah was told. "She has become pregnant through her looseness."

"Take her out and have her burned," said Judah.

Under arrest, Tamar produced Judah's cloak, seal, and staff. "I am pregnant by the man who owns these."

A dumbfounded Judah stared at his belongings and confessed: "She is more innocent than I."

The rabbis, indeed, emphasized the innocence of Tamar. In the Talmud (Megillah), Rabbi Shmuel ben-Nachmani says in the name of Rabbi Jonathan: "A bride who is chaste in the house of her father-in-law will be rewarded that kings and prophets will descend from her." From where do we learn this? From the story of Judah and Tamar: "And Judah saw her and thought her to be a whore because she had covered her face." Because (as a whore) she covered her face? Isn't it to the contrary, i.e., that he would have recognized a whore by her lack of veiled modesty? Rabbi Elazar explained: "She had covered her face when she had been in his home, therefore he did not recognize her" when she seduced him, "and therefore she was rewarded with descendants who were kings [the House of David] and prophets [Isaiah]."

The Talmud (Megillah) points to kingship and royalty as the reward for sexual modesty outside the bedroom. It is said that for her modesty, the matriarch Rachel merited that King Saul descend from her. As a reward for his modesty, King Saul merited that Esther descend from him.

And in the beginning was Tamar. She carried Judah's baby—twins, actually—to term. One of them was Peretz, ancestor of Boaz, grandfather of King David, ancestor of the Messiah. The seemingly sordid story of Judah and Tamar is a mighty measure of how forgiving and blunt the Bible is about sexuality. And these are the great-grandparents of the Messiah, yet.

What of Judah? It is said that whoever sins in private "pinches the feet of the Shechina," God's feminine aspect; but it is also recorded that Rabbi Illai the Elder taught in the Talmud (Hagigah) that "if one feels that his passion threatens to make itself master over him, he shall go to a place where he is not known, put on black clothes and do as he pleases, but he shall not profane the name of Heaven publicly." There is no contradiction here. The first case refers to someone who has found a means of checking his evil inclination; the second case deals with someone who is unable to do so. Judah falls into the second category.

The sages knew that people do all kinds of things that are not done according to the rules, regulations, or spirit of the law. But do keep a lid on the indiscretion, to whatever extent possible. Never bring a *boosha*—a shame and disgrace—on your spouse, neighbors, teachers, and religion.

On another level, it is important to note that for Judah to seek a sexual relationship outside of marriage was by no means a sin according to the Jewish laws applicable in the Genesis era. Judah was shamed because he attempted to deny responsibility, for irresponsibility is never an option. At that time concubines were an acceptable accessory for the holiest of men, including Judah's grandfather Abraham, whose concubine Hagar is perhaps the best known concubine in the Bible besides being the mother of Ishmael, said to be the forefather of the Arab peoples.

Although monogamy has for more than a millennium been the singular norm in the Jewish community, some leading sages are still making the case that the concubine relationship deserves to be reexamined. Rabbi Yakov Emden, in *Shalot Yaavetz*, writes as follows:

> Those who prefer the concubinal arrangement may certainly do so . . . for perhaps the [concubine] woman wishes to be able to leave immediately without any divorce proceedings in the event that she is mistreated, or perhaps either party is unprepared for the heavy responsibilities of marital obligations. . . . In such cases, for example, the Torah offered the option of the concubinal relationship, a relationship which is mutually initiated through oral agreement and may be terminated orally. . . . Marriage is not mandatory. [And, indeed, Judah did not marry Tamar after he admitted to fathering her child.] And those who claim that living together is a violation of a biblical commandment to marry are mistaken . . . for the Torah did not mandate marriage, only that a man be fruitful and multiply . . . and that precept may be properly fulfilled in a non-marital relationship.

As for Judah's son, Onan—poor Onan! What a fate to go through history leaving nothing but onanism, your very name, as the "ism" for masturbation. The situation with Onan is often misinterpreted. His offense was not the spilling of his seed but his avoidance of the obligation to have a child with the childless widow of his dead brother.

The sages, nevertheless, did not want men to masturbate. Because if a man can masturbate he does not need a woman. He does not have to treat her kindly or work for Shalom Bayit. He can just go away and do it by himself. And there would be fewer children in the world, fewer souls able to be put in earthly bodies to continue their transmigration through history.

Does the tradition forbid female masturbation, or women's pursuit of other lovers? Just as women were ignored and left out of most other aspects of the religio-legal restrictions, they were ignored by many of the sexual laws as well. Since the rabbis were highly exact, their silence implies that women may indeed masturbate. Still, a mode of behavior developed within the oral tradition, later codified, which elevated "sexual modesty" among a woman's primary religious obligations.

Over the centuries, the sages tried to craft a social code aimed at reducing sexual temptation. For example, they established laws prohibiting men and women from sitting alone in a room with the door closed. Even today, there are classes given in Orthodox neighborhoods to prepare men and women for any situation, with new rules adapted for new contingencies. For those who vacation in bungalow colonies, rabbis teach that a person cannot give a member of the opposite sex a ride on a country road where they might be able to easily pull over and get lost together. A man can be alone with a woman only on a superhighway where there is less chance of stopping. If a man or a woman desperately needs a ride, one of them must sit in the back seat.

The rabbis concluded that when a man and a woman are allowed to be alone, the devil makes three. Even when nothing happens, something happens. Such was the story of Joseph, Judah's younger brother. Joseph was sold by his brothers to a passing band of Midianites who in turn sold Joseph to Potiphar, an Egyptian officer. Joseph was soon promoted to the head of Potiphar's estate, with Potiphar "leaving all his affairs in Joseph's hands except for the food he himself ate." Before long, Potiphar's wife asked the "handsome and well favored" Joseph to make love to her. He refused. She attempted her seduction for days and nights. Then one day, Joseph came to Potiphar's house "to do his work." No one was home but Mrs. Potiphar. As the Bible says, "There was not a man of the household's men" to be seen. Mrs. Potiphar grabbed Joseph's cloak. "Sleep with me," she begged. Joseph ran away, leaving his ripped cloak in her hand. He asked, "How can I do this wickedness and sin against God?"

Nevertheless, with Joseph's clothes as evidence—she caressed them as if they were his skin, crying into the cloth—Mrs. Potiphar told everyone, including her husband, that Joseph had tried to rape her, that he had teased and toyed with her for weeks. Joseph was thrown in jail. He languished there until his skill at interpreting dreams earned him a pardon from the pharaoh.

A key lesson from this story is that sexuality and sensuality take place in the brain. No one is helpless or unable to say "no" unless under extraordinary duress. To the Bible, as well as to Joseph, the seductive woman never was identified by her individual name. She was always Mrs. Potiphar—another man's wife.

Joseph is known in the tradition as Joseph the Tzaddik, the Righteous One, primarily because of his mastery of his sexual desires. The Torah contains more biographical detail about him than about any other person except for Moses. The classic rabbinic commentaries dwell on how handsome he was. He was a snazzy dresser, as famous for his coat of many colors as anything else.

Why such interest in Joseph? Elie Wiesel writes that "modesty between the sexes is supposed to be a Jewish virtue, so that logically the Talmud should have spared the reader" its vast speculation on Joseph's sexual magnetism. "However," notes Wiesel, "the opposite is true: the reader is treated to scene upon scene, with only slight variations, illustrating the ravages wreaked by Joseph in the hearts of Egyptian womanhood."

Some sages suggested that Joseph was in fact naked, aroused, and in bed with Mrs. Potiphar but restrained himself when the image of Father Jacob appeared before him. This suggests a holy impotence accompanied by spiritual potency brought about by psychological factors, the reawakening of his father's teachings.

Another suggestion of impotency comes from the Bible telling us that before Joseph went into the house of Potiphar, "none of the men of the house were within," which could be a simple statement of the building's occupancy, or it could refer to absence of her sexual servants as well as the descent of Joseph's masculine urges with the ascent of his sense of right and wrong. We know by now that the Bible and the Talmudic commentary are not shy. If anything would have happened between Joseph and Mrs. Potiphar, we would surely have been told. Instead we are told that even in a land of rampant hedonism, sexual freedom, and self-gratification, Joseph understood that there is such a thing as a sin, that God is a witness when there is no other.

It is interesting to note that although Potiphar's wife charged Joseph with rape, he was imprisoned with political and ideological prisoners such as deposed officers from the pharaoh's court, not common criminals or other rapists.

Joseph's self-control became a model for the ages. According to the Talmud (Yoma):

> The wicked man will be asked at the Divine Judgment why he did not study Torah. If he answers that he was too handsome and tempted by his inclinations, they will answer him,

was he more tempted than Joseph the Righteous? It was said of Joseph that every day Potiphar's wife used to try and seduce him by her talk. The clothes she used to put on in the morning she did not put on in the evening.

The Joseph story is also invoked by the rabbis as an example of the necessity for precautionary modesty. It is written in the Talmud (Brachot) that "a man should avoid appointing a supervisor over his household, for had not Potiphar appointed Joseph supervisor over his household [then the trouble with Potiphar's wife] would not have occurred."

Joseph's and Judah's sister Dina was somewhat less successful in her adventures beyond her tribal tents. In Genesis we are told that Dina "went out among the daughters of the land," seeking anonymity far from her family. A prince by the name of Shechem saw her and made love to her. The Bible says, "His soul was drawn to Dina; he loved her and spoke tenderly to her." He wanted to marry her. Simon and Levy, Dina's other brothers, were furious and plotted to avenge the prince's violation of their sister. They said they would allow the marriage if Shechem and his family would convert to the religion of Abraham, and get circumcised.

While Shechem and his men were incapacitated from their newly performed circumcisions, Simon and Levy came with their swords and murdered Shechem and all his men, as if to say, "When you came to our sister, you acted with your penis, so while you are incapacitated because of your penis, we will avenge our sister's honor." When Jacob heard of this he was furious, but the Bible gives the brothers the last word: "Shall our sister be treated like a whore?"

In the Biblical text we are told nothing, absolutely nothing, about Dina's life except for the incident with Shechem, and even there we are not told how she felt about Shechem, whether his words of love were accepted by her, or whether she considered herself raped. Some commentators approached the issue by noting that just as Dina was ignored by her family, leading to her excursion to the wild side "with the daughters of the land," so she was ignored later, when her feelings remained secondary to family honor.

Why does the Torah tell us about a family like Jacob's in which there are so many problems? And why does the Torah not even bother to tell us about Joseph's theology, or Judah's?

The author of Genesis knew human nature, knew that these things do happen in families. He does not suggest that a person or family is precluded from future greatness because of a sordid past. Indeed, it is what we do with our future that counts, that decides whether Judah and Tamar's out-of-wedlock child becomes a detriment to society or the messianic ancestor.

The original, primal depiction of the Messiah has evolved through the years. But the messianic lineage in Genesis is pockmarked with sexual affairs that seem to invite scorn, whereas the classical Christian model and some later rabbis chose to emphasize the messiah's purity, freedom from sin, and lack of sexuality.

Not only does the Jewish Bible, moreover, stress the Messiah's genealogy from Lot's daughters and Tamar, but from Ruth, who crept into the granary in the dark of night to sleep with Boaz. What all three events—Lot's daughter, Tamar, and Ruth—have in common, says Rabbi Irving "Yitz" Greenberg, quoting rabbinic masters, is three women whose commitment to life is so elemental, whose unquenchable faith runs so deep, that they would stop at nothing to ensure life and continuity. Lot's daughters, believing that no more men were left, got their father drunk to procreate, to further life.

That was Tamar's reasoning, as well, when she kept trying to have a child with Judah's sons and later with Judah himself. She would simply not give in to death. It was Ruth's as well. Ruth, a childless widow, was determined that life go on. The Messiah in the Jewish tradition is the elemental life force that will stop at nothing.

Current generations of Jews have witnessed the overwhelming onslaught of death during World War II and in one horror after another since then. Perhaps, like these Biblical women, the erotic reawakening that accompanied the State of Israel's rebirth indicates that Jews today feel an overwhelming need to reaffirm life and its sexual force which gives so much joy.

The kabbalists, masters of the Jewish mystical tradition, did not like the idea of any love affair not having a happy ending. They too would not give in to death as the end of any story. According to the kabbalists, when Shechem died it was not the end of the story—only the beginning.

The Kabbalah, in the book called Sefer Ha-Gilgulim (the book explaining the Jewish belief in reincarnation and life after death), says that Dina and Shechem returned to this world several generations later, when the Israelites were wandering through the desert. Only this time, she returned as a he—Zimri, a Jewish prince descended from brother Simon. As for Shechem, he returned as a she—Cosbi, a non-Jewish Midianite princess.

Again, they were accused of being illicit. And while Cosbi and Zimri were making love in public—in defiance of the recently given laws at Sinai—Pinchas the Priest (a grandson of Aaron and grandnephew of Moses) speared them both through the genitals, to their death. This is quite similar to the way Shechem was killed—also in a way relating to his genitals, as he was recovering from a circumcision.

But while the Torah explicitly says that God approved this murder in retaliation for sexual brazenness that threatened the moral and ethnic cohesiveness of the Jews in the Sinai desert, the Jewish mystical tradition adds a romantic footnote. The Kabbalists write that the souls of Dina/Zimri and Shechem/Cosbi returned one more time—this time in the Talmudic era as the great Rabbi Akiba and the wife of Tyranus Rufus, the Roman governor. The ancient souls are given yet another chance to correct the sexual affairs and weaknesses of centuries past. Now Tyranus Rufus sent his wife to seduce Akiba, to prove that this saintly Akiba was not such a saint after all. Obviously, this is a common scheme through the centuries—scoundrels trying to prove that the saintly are scoundrels as well.

But the Kabbalah tells us that when Akiba saw the wife of the Roman governor, "He laughed, he cried, and he spit."

"He laughed." Through the gift of prophecy he knows that after his own wife dies, and after the Roman governor dies, he would marry and make love to this beautiful seductress, ending the most amazing coitus interruptus in human history—an intercourse carried from Dina in the antiquity of time to Zimri in the time of Moses to Akiba in the time of the Romans!

"He cried." Akiba breaks down remembering the spiritual and sexual frustrations of these previous incarnations. He actually feels the sadness of knowing that once more such a beautiful woman would know death (even if through natural causes).

"And he spit." Akiba had contempt for the fact that his lover, his eternal soulmate, should be reduced to being the wife of an immoral Roman governor, an enemy of Akiba's people.

But today, of course, poor souls are lucky enough to have sex therapists. We are closer to the end of days, say the rabbis, and we don't have time for souls to keep shlepping their problems across the centuries. Souls have to get their sex lives on track immediately.

The Kabbalah teaches us that what sometimes appears to be sinful is actually holy in worlds that we cannot see. If something doesn't work, God will keep bringing the couple back until they get it right, even if it takes a millennium. What a different and opposite approach this is from those who preach that a couple will burn in hell forever for a singular transgression.

Along these lines, the traditional Jewish greeting is *Shalom Aleichem,* which is plural. And even if we are greeting just one person, we say "shalom aleichem" anyway, indicative of the Jewish belief that one person is a community unto him or herself, carrying the soul of many others that came before. For example, when we meet Akiba, we are meeting Dina and Zimri: "Shalom aleichem, peace onto all of you."

According to the Jewish tradition, no sexual relationship is as simple as it seems on the surface; the puritanical sexual attitude often attributed to religion is only supportable when the Bible is read on the most simple and superficial of levels.

The sages say that a scholar must be at least forty years old, married, and a father before he is qualified to study Kabbalah, the inner secrets of the Bible. The Kabbalah is so inherently sexual that unless someone has had sexual experience themselves and has been around long enough to confront the mysteries of sex, it is almost impossible for him to understand God's Book and the forces of creation. This level of sex education is not for the yeshiva boy-under-the-bed. This is graduate school.

Now let us suppose that some actual Dina or Tamar comes to my office, a nice Jewish girl from a nice Jewish family who was indeed the victim of a negative sexual situation. What is most helpful from the Torah stories is the understanding that unfortunate situations do occur and must be talked about. The Torah illustrates that these things happen in the nicest families, in the holiest of families. Life not only can and must go on, but redemption is ever present and ever possible.

When an Orthodox girl sits in my office and tells me that something troubling has happened to her, I tell her from the depth of my Jewish tradition: "What happened is terrible, just awful, it should never have happened to a person like you. What a pity that you have had to have that bad experience. But you must get on with life. When the memory or the thought pops up in your mind, let's make sure you redeem it with some good thoughts. Think about Miriam going out with her tambourine and dancing after the crossing of the Red Sea, when all seemed hopeless. Think about the Shabbos candles and the havdalah as the holy flames intertwine. Put that into your mind along with the wishes of God and the person that you are involved with right now."

As for a religious woman or man who is involved in a relationship where the partner is sexually satisfying but is a bad life partner, I would advise the person to remember the magicians of Egypt. When Moses came to Pharaoh, he attempted to show that he was God's representative by performing special signs and miracles. But everything that

Moses was able to do, Pharaoh's magicians were able to duplicate.

We know that there is no biological difference between sex with an abuser and sex with a lover. The difference is emotional and spiritual. Just as Moses and the magicians performed the same act but with different motivations—as did Tamar, Ruth, and other Bible characters—it becomes evident that one person can use sex and the appearance of love to keep you enslaved, while another can use sex and love to be your redeemer, setting you free.

Three

"Thou Shalt Not . . ."

A story from the tractate Sanhedrin, told by Rabbi Judah in the name of Rav: A man once developed a powerful sexual obsession for a woman. His heart was so consumed by his burning desire that his life was supposedly endangered. Doctors were consulted. They said the man's trouble was innate, not his fault, it was genetic, medical, biological, psychological. There was no cure other than the woman submitting to him. At which point the sages said, "Let him die before she should have to submit."

The doctors said, "At least let her stand nude before him." The sages replied, "Sooner let him die."

"Then," said the doctors, "let him converse with her from behind a partition." "Let him die," said the sages.

Other rabbis asked, "Is the woman in question married or not?" One said that the sages' severity could only make sense if she were married. If she were not married, then why could he not marry her? Rabbi Papa said, "Because of the disgrace to her family." Rabbi Aha, the son of Rabbi Ika, said that marriage under such circumstances was unthinkable, "That the daughters of Israel may not be morally dissolute."

The sages said of the obsessed man, "Marriage will not assuage his passion," for, as Rabbi Isaac said, "Since the destruction of the Temple, sexual pleasure has been taken from the lawful and given to sinners, as it is written in the Book of Proverbs, 'Stolen waters are sweet, and bread eaten in secret is pleasant.' "

Perhaps Jewish sovereignty in Jerusalem for the first time since the Temple days has contributed to the lawful reclamation of sexual pleasure, but there is no doubt that much of the sexual culture to this day thrives on the illicit, the thrill of danger, the sense that sexual passion indeed cannot be contained only in marriage. And it is almost a cliché—perhaps fueled by the dominant Christian culture's association of religion with puritans, the celibacy of Jesus, and the Catholic Church—that sexual pleasure has indeed been taken from the "lawful and given to sinners," as the Talmud itself declares. (The First Temple was built during the reign of King Solomon, 965 B.C.E., and it was destroyed almost four centuries later in 586 B.C.E. Seventy years later, the Second Temple was inaugurated and it lasted until the year 70 of the common era. The first rabbinic discourses to be included in the central Babylonian Talmud began appearing the first century of the common era, and canonization occurred in the sixth century.)

The Talmud considered the destruction of the two temples—sometimes condensing the tale of mourning of the Second Temple into that of the more glorious First—which marked the end of Jewish sovereignty for two thousand years, to be the most cataclysmic event in Jewish history. It was treated in rabbinic literature with the severity and solemnity accorded to the Holocaust today. The Hebrew words for the Holocaust, "Shoah" and "Hoorbahn," were used for two millennia to refer to the twin destructions and to the events leading to the vast and enduring exile, which theologically still exists—because the State of Israel is a political enterprise that has not ushered in a messianic era and the building of a Third Temple.

In this context, everything that occurred before the ancient Shoah is considered superior—even the sex had by the rabbis, "the lawful"—than anything that has come after. But a growing number of modern rabbis say that the return of the Israelite descendants to sovereignty in the Holy Land is certainly, at the very least, a messianic harbinger. The fact that hundreds of thousands of rabbis and traditional Jews are taking delight in sexual pleasure is another robin of spring to those who say that the geographic and spiritual exile are drawing to a close. However, without wishing to be disrespectful, I feel that the lawful sexual activity enjoyed by Kings David and Solomon, as documented in the Bible and in their own literature such as the Song of Songs, is clearly beyond any sexual documentation about post-Temple heads of state or prime ministers, so maybe the Talmud is on to something after all.

Nevertheless, it is totally wrong to think that David and Solomon lived outside any sexual rules or checks and balances. When David spies Batsheva bathing on a rooftop and arranges for her husband to die in battle so he could take her as one of his wives, he was rebuked by Prophet Nathan, and more amazingly repented in public. This at a time in antiquity when kings generally answered to no one and took the women of their nation as the royal eminent domain.

The sages say that King Solomon was the wisest man of all, and the author of three books in the Bible—Ecclesiastes, Song of Songs, and Proverbs. And yet, the destruction of the Second Temple by the Romans was blamed by the rabbis on Solomon's sexual indiscretions: Rabbi Isaac said in the tractate Sanhedrin that "when Solomon married the daughter of Pharaoh, the Angel Gabriel came down and stuck a reed into the sea, and it gathered about itself on a bank upon which the great city of Rome was built."

King Hezekiah, from the House of David, was another Biblical king, a contemporary of Prophet Isaiah. Hezekiah, who was not celibate, was said to have been a potential messiah but was deprived because he never sang; one sage actually said he was the savior. Hezekiah, says the Talmud (in tractate Brachot), became deathly ill and was visited by Isaiah, who told him he was subject to a most severe punishment: to die in this world and be deprived of the World to Come. When the king asked why, Isaiah answered with words uttered by Jewish parents from Babylonia to Poland to Brooklyn through the centuries: "Because you have not married," said Isaiah.

"Aye," said Hezekiah, "it was because I saw through the Divine spirit that bad children will come forth from me."

"What have you to do with the secrets of the Almighty?" replied Isaiah. "Whatever you are commanded to do, you ought to fulfill, and whatever pleases the Holy One, let Him do." It didn't matter in the least that Hezekiah was the king; he broke the exalted procreation commandments and he was to be punished.

The sages demanded that the Israelites and their kings marry. The Talmud's Rav Nachman said in the name of Samuel, in tractate Yebamos, that "although a man has many children he is nevertheless prohibited from remaining single" in the event of his wife's death or divorce. Rabbi Joshua says: "Although a man took a wife while he was young, he should nevertheless marry again (if he is alone) when he becomes old. Although one has children from his early years, he should also try to have children when he is old, as it is written (Ecclesiastes 11:6): 'In the morning sow your seed, and in the evening let not your hand rest, for you do not know if you will succeed, whether this or that or both will be equally good.' "

Rabbi Elazar said, "A Jewish [man] who does not have a wife is not a man. . . . Adam did not find life satisfying until Eve was brought to him."

And a king had to marry for the protection of his subjects. Rabbi Chama ben-Chanina says, "As soon as a man is married his sins stop accusing him, for it is said in the Book of Proverbs: 'Who has found a wife has found happiness and has obtained favor from the Lord.' "

Rabbi Elazar says, "Every Jew who does not marry is considered as one who sheds blood." There was a saying in ancient Israel that "he (who is unmarried) is without Torah and without protection." The Talmud (tractate Brachot) states that a handsome wife helps develop the mind of a man.

But rebuke and the Temple's destruction were lain not only at the feet of Israel's royalty. The following story is told by the Talmud that blames the sexual mores of the commoners.

It happened that a carpenter fell in love with his employer's wife. Once, when his employer was in need of money, the carpenter said: "Give me your wife and I will send you the money you need." The employer gave his wife for the money. After three days, the employer came to repay the money and take back his wife. The carpenter said, "I sent her home but I heard that highwaymen captured her while she was on the road."

"What should I do?" asked the husband.

"Divorce her," said the carpenter.

"But how can I?" asked the husband. "Her dowry was for a substantial amount of money."

"I'll lend you the money," said the carpenter.

The husband divorced his wife. The carpenter married her. When the time came to repay the loan, the first husband could not do so, and he was forced to work as an indentured servant to the carpenter. While the new husband and wife were sitting, eating, and drinking, the former husband served them as tears fell from his eyes into the goblet he was carrying to the carpenter.

"At this moment," say the sages, "a decree was passed in Heaven that Jerusalem would be destroyed."

It is not that the good citizens of ancient Israel did not resist. They did, and what provoked them to rebellion was not excessive taxation or brutal politics, but the disrespect shown by the Romans for the traditional Jewish customs regarding procreation and Jewish weddings.

In the town of Tura Malka it was customary that when a bride and groom were escorted to their wedding, the people would dance to their happiness with a hen and a rooster, the idea being that the new couple should multiply like fowl. Once, at such a wedding, Roman soldiers passing by took away the hen and the rooster. The people attacked the soldiers and beat them to a pulp. The soldiers reported the incident as a rebellion against Caesar. The Romans then laid waste to the land.

A similar legend comes from the Israeli town of Betar. An ancient custom there dictated that when a child was born the parents would plant a cedar tree for a boy, a pine tree for a girl. They would later cut down the trees for use as a wedding canopy. One day the daughter of the Roman emperor was riding through the city when her carriage shaft broke. Her attendants cut down a nearby cedar to repair it. The father who planted the cedar for his child's wedding canopy attacked the attendants and beat them. They informed Caesar that this attack was part of a rebellion. He immediately dispatched a great army, and the inhabitants of the city were massacred.

There was other resistance to the assault on Jewish sexual ethics. It is said that four hundred boys and girls were kidnapped aboard a ship and targeted for use in a sexually shameful way. When the young prisoners learned the purpose of their capture, they jumped into the sea and drowned.

Although the Jewish tradition is notable for its general openness to sexuality, such openness should not be confused with laissez-faire permissiveness. The Torah in the eighteenth chapter of Leviticus is quite explicit—at least for men—as to what relationships are not only forbidden but labeled perverse and abominable.

The Bible states that it is forbidden to have sex with your

- Father or mother
- Father's wife
- Sister, even if she is the daughter of only one parent, whether she is legitimate or illegitimate
- Granddaughter
- Aunt
- Brother's wife
- Daughter-in-law
- Wife's sister, as long as your wife is alive
- Neighbor's wife

One may also not sleep with

- A daughter that your father's wife has borne to your father

- A woman and her daughter, or a woman and her granddaughter
- A woman who is menstruating

A man may not have sex with another man as he would with a woman "for this is a disgusting abomination." Nor may one perform any sexual act with an animal, "since it will defile you. A woman shall not give herself to an animal and allow it to mate with her. This is an utterly detestable perversion." The Bible warns, "Whenever anyone does any of these disgusting perversions, [all] the people involved shall be cut off from the midst of their people."

It is important to note that these laws are addressed to men, for the most part, rather than to women. However, Rabbi Schneur Zalman, the first Lubavitcher rebbe, pointed out that there is yet a key Jewish axiom of sexual propriety: "What is prohibited is forbidden, but not all that is permissible is necessary." There are many activities that are kosher but are spiritually unacceptable, such as relationships that are hurtful to third parties, or relationships in which the power is unequal and one person is using the other. There is no point, the first Lubavitcher rebbe argues, in aspiring to holiness while looking for loopholes.

Not everything that is thought has to be said, not everything that is felt must be acted upon, and not every object of desire must be acquired, say the rabbis. Indeed, according to the tradition, as God is concerned for all His children, every person created in God's image must likewise be concerned for all others who, of course, are also created in God's image. The Talmud, using hyperbole for dramatic emphasis, states that to humiliate or embarrass another is analogous to murder. There is a sense among many who live traditional Jewish lives that just as a corral is built to keep in the cattle, a fence of physical and verbal modesty must be built as well, to corral our coarser selves.

All of the Leviticus prohibitions have become cultural taboos in cultures far beyond the original Twelve Tribes of Israel who accepted these laws at the foot of Mount Sinai.

Some say that Judaism virtually "invented" homophobia, as well as many of these prohibitions, because in the ancient world sexuality was not segmented by orientation or variation. Hammurabi, author of the ancient world's most famous pre-Biblical legal codes, had male lovers. The Greeks and Romans glorified homosexuality, and man-boy love was nothing out of the ordinary. The Jewish Bible was the first known document that challenged the pagan notion that sex was an act divorced from the soul or from spiritual consequences. And by insisting on male-female relationships as the only sanctified norm, Judaism began the civilizing process of elevating those within a procreative relationship. With the passing of the centuries, the rabbinate has moved on one religio-legal front after another to secure the status of women, especially by moving to limit even the Biblical allowance of polygamy and concubines.

Jewish law allows for change and amendments, even for laws ordained by God in the explicit fashion. For example, although the Torah is quite definite about not allowing any leavened bread to even be possessed on Passover, the sages crafted a legal fiction in which a Jew may sell his leavened goods to a non-Jew who then sells it back to the Jew after Passover. Yet the laws of sexuality and the categorizing of perversions remained immune to any amendment for more than three thousand years. Even the Talmudic divorce laws, considered archaic even by many Orthodox rabbis, have for the most part eluded amendment.

It is no surprise, then, to Jewish legal scholars that the most well-intentioned and sincere entreaties by gay activists have run into a wall. Amending Jewish law is all the more difficult in modern times when, without a universally recognized law-making body such as existed in antiquity, Jewish factionalism precludes any one group from having the authority to act for the collective religion, even assuming they would have the inclination.

The problem exists primarily for Orthodox and traditional Conservative Jews who attempt to legislate according to talmudic guidelines; the Reform and Reconstructionist rabbinical groups do not claim fidelity to traditional Jewish law nor to the Divine origins of Biblical commandments. They assert that Jewish tradition has a vote but not a veto over modern rabbinic policy. The Orthodox grant tradition a very definite veto to the point where it is unclear at times whether anyone else has even a vote at all.

Where change has been allowed, in the more traditional camp, it has only done so in cases that glorify the ascension of the monogamous male-female ideal. Jewish legalists say that like all legal systems, it is fueled by legal precedent and interpretations of the group's constitution—the Bible. The Bible's intent may be ascertained, they say, by the fact that there are hundreds of analogies in the Bible to the God-Israel relationship as paralleling husband-wife love. When God and the Israelites grow estranged, the analogy given numerous times in the Books of the Prophets is to an unfaithful wife or to a harlot, metaphors that stay within the confines of heterosexuality. There is not a single analogy to homosexual love, nor is there an example of the other Levitical laws ever having been defied or disowned in any later Biblical or Talmudic era.

Among traditional Jews, the eradication of any of these laws is unthinkable, and there is resentment toward those untraditional Jews who do not accept the foundations and assumptions of traditional Jewish law in the first place, but nevertheless agitate for change in the sexual legislation.

Traditional Jews, who read aloud from the Torah at least three times a week, believe that the Torah's every word is equated with the word of God, leaving homosexuality deep within the closet. Therefore, very few Jews have been able to become actively and openly homosexual without having to sever ties to the traditional Jewish community.

To even the most modern of traditional Jews, this dilemma seems unfortunate. But this is no more so than when another traditional Jew becomes a connoisseur of fine, nonkosher wine and is then forced to choose between his palate and his traditional community. According to Jewish law, personal desire, addiction, or predisposition is not an alibi for an unkosher choice. God's word is God's word, and so the traditional Jew resents being called homophobic, when in fact he is helpless when forced to choose between several millennia of belief and a philosophy of sexual permissiveness that seems relatively pagan at worst and hardly tested in its spiritual repercussions at best.

Phobia has nothing to do with it; the Bible has everything to do with it. Despite the massive social agitation from the secular world and liberal Jews, it remains a simple and blunt fact that the traditional rabbinates in both the Orthodox and Conservative movements do not condone any homosexual or lesbian acts. As of this writing, no openly homosexual or lesbian Jew, no matter how otherwise pious, is allowed even to be matriculated within any Orthodox or Conservative seminary, let alone be ordained, though homosexuals are accepted to the Reform rabbinate. As we are concerning ourselves with traditional Judaism, we must acknowledge the situation as it is.

In the traditional world, the approach most often taken is to love the sinner while hating the sin—an unacceptable compromise to most gay activists. Although most opposition to the acceptance of homosexuality, socially as well as legally, is associated with the Orthodox, the Conservative movement has taken several stands that are worth mentioning. At rabbinic conventions it is frequently reiterated that Conservative Jews support full civil equality for homosexuals and condemn violence against gays. Opposition is limited to within the religious arena, such as sanctifying a gay marriage, for example, which is considered a mockery of Jewish law, reducing Judaism to celebratory theater rather than a serious theology. The vast majority of modern rabbis will also not officiate at heterosexual marriages between a Jew and a non-Jew. In the State of Israel, civic law recognizes Orthodox rabbinic law on matters of personal status, such as weddings.

In 1992, the Conservative movement's Committee on Jewish Law and Standards said that although openly gay Jews may not become rabbis (as may not anyone else who openly violates existing Jewish law), gays may be accepted to congregational membership, summer camps, youth groups, and schools.

While the Orthodox Union, the most mainstream Orthodox synagogue movement, condemns civic discrimination as well as homosexuality, other Orthodox groups have expressed the fear that relaxing any of the cultural barriers invariably leads to an environment conducive to the sin of homosexuality.

As evidenced by the forbidden list in Leviticus, traditional Jews who observe every letter of the Bible have no recourse to modernity's increasing acceptance of homosexuality, no more than they would of bestiality or incest.

Traditional Jewish culture as it is now constituted, especially in the yeshiva and in the Hasidic world, is perhaps the most homosocial—men socializing with men, women with women—in American society. In those circumstances, writes Alisa Solomon in the *Village Voice,* "homosexual panic is bound to be greater."

Another critique comes from former *New York Times* religion correspondent Ari Goldman, who, in his book *The Search for God at Harvard,* writes that homosexuality is the dark secret of the yeshiva world in which young men—deprived of anything more than minimal contact with non-familial women—live, study, eat, breathe, and even bathe with their fellow yeshiva students while in the prime of their sexual development.

Indeed, in the rabbinic text Avot d'Rabbi Natan, it is written, "K'nai lecha chaver" (acquire a friend). This means that a person "should set himself a companion, to eat with him, drink with him, study Bible with him, study Mishna with him, *sleep with him,* and reveal to him all secrets, secrets of Torah and secrets of worldly things." Does sleep mean sex or familial brotherhood?

There has yet to be a yeshiva in the history of Judaism that has encouraged students to sleep with their classmates, and there has yet to be a rabbi who interpreted any text in any but a heterosexual manner.

Nevertheless, Dr. Abba Borowich, an Orthodox psychiatrist, told an interviewer at *Moment,* a Jewish journal, that he has treated numerous Orthodox homosexuals, mostly from the more sexually separatist sects. "The reason," says Borowich, "is that there is no other outlet for them. The boys are segregated from the girls and they are forbidden to masturbate. Homosexual activity fulfills the role of masturbation for them." Rarely, though, does this teenage experimentation extend into adulthood or into marriage.

The awesome prohibition against touching a woman, let alone socializing with her, has led to a popular Orthodox joke. *Q:* Why is sleeping with a woman prohibited? *A:* It might lead to mixed-dancing. "Mixed-dancing," men dancing with women, might be a confusing term to those unfamiliar with this culture. It is what the non-Orthodox would refer to as touch dancing or ballroom standards. But to traditional Jews, proper dancing is what happens at weddings, where men dance with men in a wide circle, and women dance with women. A whole new slang has to develop to mediate between what something might mean "on the inside" or to outsiders.

Borowich says that yeshiva homosexuals "hide it the best they can. But sometimes they get into trouble with fellow hasidim in the mikvah [ritual pool] or even by carrying their homosexuality [into something less episodic]. They may seek out sex [telephone] lines or male prostitutes."

Solomon claims that "homosexuality riles the Jewish American imagination." Much of American anti-Semitism is often expressed, she says, "in stereotypes of Jews as gender-dysfunctional: the effeminate, wimpy man; the woman who's not really a woman either because she's a commandeering Jewish mother or, a generation later, a frigid but highly adorned Jewish American Princess. Meanwhile, the stereo-typical Jewish family—meek father, always away at work; domineering mother, always in the kitchen—is exactly the stereotype of the sort of parents who produce gay sons."

Orthodox men are trained to be unapologetic about their masculinity. In the streets and in the synagogues' prayer halls they wear their black fedoras at jaunty angles and thank God every morning in daily prayer for not having been made a woman. Orthodox women, who at least early in marriage may be the economic providers while the men attend to study, are less cloistered and have fewer incidents of sapphic indiscretion. Their morning prayer is less confrontational, thanking God "for making me according to Thy will."

The weak father/strong mother stereotype has suffered a major blow in the latter half of this century, as the Orthodox world has become triumphalist and Zionism has taken its place among the dominant clarion calls of Jewish awareness. David Biale, author of *Eros and the Jews,* calls Zionism the "erotic revolution," in that it replaced the myth of the Jewish tailor and money-lender with the myth of the pioneer farmer-soldier who wins wars as if by superhuman skill. After the 1967 Six Day War, one of the best-selling posters portrayed a typical weak eastern European Jew entering a phone booth and changing into Super Jew.

In Israel, there are now thousands of Orthodox yeshiva students who go through the Israeli army's rigorous basic training as well as fight on the front lines if need be. As Solomon says, "Zionism has been defined as the means by which Jews (at least Jewish men) acquired not only a home-land but a body." Jackie Mason often jokes that young Israeli men look like Puerto Ricans, lean and tough, not like the Jews the comedian remembers from his pre-Israel youth.

But this eroticism is contained within the confines of Torah law. Biale has written in *Tikkun* magazine that categories such as "repression" and "gratification" are uniquely modern and may not be relevant to this tradition. According to those who live by the Bible, certain foods are not available to our culinary appetites and certain people are not available for our sexual appetites, although these unavailable people may serve as stimulants.

A traditional Jew may fully be aware that certain unkosher foods may be delicious, and those who enjoy such foods may be good people. Further, a traditional Jew may even yearn to taste a lobster or a cheeseburger. This does not earn the yearning Jew the designation of someone who is "not kosher." Even eating the lobster or the cheeseburger does not make the person kosher or unkosher. It is the lobster that is not kosher, not the individual. The person who just swallowed the lobster does not acquire any special status as a nonkosher Jew, beyond the singular sin in that singular moment. Similarly, one who commits a sexual wrongdoing, that person does not acquire any particular permanent or semipermanent status, such as being "gay." The noun "homosexual" simply did not exist in Biblical Hebrew.

Biale's central argument is that Leviticus cannot be dismissed as repressive any more than its sister Biblical volume, the Song of Songs, may be distorted as licentious. Rather, he says, the tradition is about "the dilemmas of desire, the struggle between contradictory attractions. . . . The Bible, in all its complexity, is concerned primarily with a theology of procreation," an emphasis on what some call "sacred sex" that must parallel safe sex, sacred sex being a behavior whose aim is a stellar standard of behavior in line with a holy tradition, rather than expending all one's energies on little more than the sheer avoidance of pregnancy or disease. Indeed, the traditional emphasis is on promoting pregnancy.

The Jewish concept of what is sacred and sanctified is expressed through separation and designation. Sex was to flourish within boundaries, and within those boundaries the greatest eroticism was to be not only allowed but given God's blessing.

Safe sex and sacred sex are not opposite but complementary. A lover, attempting to live a life in accord with God as well as his or her love partner, will, for example, be honest and caring to avoid the spread of disease. Here, the heart, soul, and brain are as important as the penis or the vagina.

Dennis Prager, the multimedia philosopher and coauthor of *The Nine Questions People Ask About Judaism,* a perennial best-selling introduction to Judaism, writes in his journal, *Ultimate Issues:*

> Man's nature, undisciplined by values, will allow sex to dominate his life and the life of society. When Judaism demanded that all sexual activity be channeled into marriage, it changed the world. . . . This revolution consisted of forcing the sexual genie into the marital bottle. It ensured that sex no longer dominate society, heightened male-female love and sexuality—and thereby almost alone created the possibility of love and eroticism within marriage.

The Jewish tradition dismisses the idea that someone is helpless in the face of their sexual desires. Rabbi Abraham Twersky, a Hasidic psychiatrist, writes in his essays on the weekly Torah readings that "secular wisdom has developed a concept of 'irresistible impulse' which has legal implications and can be used as a mitigating factor or enough of a factor to completely exonerate one from responsibility for

[even] a criminal act. This concept is totally alien to the Torah, which rejects condoning loss of control. No circumstances, however stressful they may be, can justify loss of control."

As the sages point out on numerous occasions, the underlying assumption of the Torah is that God will not decree a law unless human beings have the capability to live by it. According to Twersky, for example, "Secular psychology often tends to minimize a person's capacity for self-mastery. Some of this is due to Freudian psychology's implication that repression of one's feelings, thoughts and drives is the root of many emotional disorders. It may appear to follow that if repression is the cause of emotional illness, then free expression should be the road to emotional health. . . . To the contrary, the appropriate response should be conscious control."

But for the traditional Jew, theories and philosophies are simply parlor games. Debating the Bible's sexual laws are as much of a dead end as debating whether the Sabbath should be changed to Wednesday.

What of the argument that homosexuals "can't help it," that they are born that way, genetically predisposed to lovers of the same sex? Whether future scientific discoveries will sustain that argument remains to be seen, and given the ping-pong of contradictory studies—all hailed as scientific and conclusive, only to be humbled by yet other studies, equally scientific—the traditional community deems it best to act with something other than haste.

A greater question confronting the traditional Jewish community is not what to do with those who are genetically disposed to sinful sexual choices, but whether homosexuality—for example, as a path of sexual experimentation for a heterosexual or bisexual—is morally neutral. The answer, according to the Jewish tradition, is a blunt "no."

From a practical therapeutic perspective, when an Orthodox Jewish man comes into my office and says he is attracted to other men, I ask him, "In your fantasies, can you imagine being with a woman? Can you feel some arousal?" If he says yes but he is also attracted to men, I tell him, "Keep your mouth shut. There is no point in telling that to anyone, and there is no recovering in the traditional community from such a self-advertisement. Jews do not have ritual confession. Do not confide. Even if it is a burden on you. When you feel aroused homosexually, try to place the image of a woman in your mind." I refer back to the story of Joseph, about whom it is written that he "was not a man," that is, he lost his erection when the image of his father's face appeared before him to warn him that Potiphar's wife, a married woman, was forbidden to him. That is how I teach about the power of the mind in terms of issues of sexuality. But when working with a patient, a doctor must work within the reasonable restrictions of the patient's culture. It is not for a therapist to "out" a patient who is unprepared for the complete and irreversible upheaval that will follow. Additionally, in non-Orthodox Western culture, a therapist would never encourage a patient to fulfill his fantasies of bestiality or sleeping with his father's wife or many other things that are forbidden on the Leviticus list.

It is a delicate matter to move a patient in a direction that the person may not be able to master. But if a traditional Jew with gay fantasies has to be married, and if throughout life he must place pictures of men into his mind in order to be aroused, difficult or painful as this may be, so be it. Fantasy is a powerful device. Sometimes, although this has not been proven, the libido is so strong that just the act of having sex takes over and sex is then enjoyed in a heterosexual context.

If he can be aroused by a door or a chair, so be it; the greater emphasis must be on the fact of arousal and a functioning sexual relationship within marriage, as that is a must within the tradition.

There is a certain amount of control that people have over their arousal. I'm not talking about someone who absolutely cannot achieve an erection with a woman. I'm talking about someone who has never had sex and is attracted to men. If that man desires a cure—and virtually all yeshiva students with this problem do so desire a cure—he can make himself, via his mind, to be sexually functional with a woman. Whether any of this is fair to the women married to these men is another matter.

Women have their own issues. I have had many traditional women in my practice who feel guilty about their lesbian desires, although the Torah is surprisingly silent on the subject. Others feel guilty over excessive sexual thought. I remind them that when the Israelites were in the desert, God told Moses to accept the beauty mirrors as gifts from the women for the Sanctuary. Some men objected to mirrors, objects of vanity. But, we are told, the Israelite male slaves were so broken by their excessive labor and by the idea that any new son would be thrown into the Nile that they frequently became impotent or withdrew from sexual relationships with their wives. These mirrors then earned their holiness: the women used the mirrors to beautify themselves before seducing their husbands and arousing them to the point where anything but freedom was inconceivable.

I try to alleviate guilt among my traditional clientele by reminding them that in the Jewish tradition guilt only relates to action. For women, as for men, fantasy is a gift from God, a safety valve. I advise each woman and man, however, not to tell their spouse that while they are making love the thoughts of another are on their mind. As long as fantasy is successful when needed, it should be given a chance.

It is useful to remind Orthodox patients that God's Torah is remarkably forgiving to sexual weaknesses, lapses, and deviations, as we see from the stories of Judah and Tamar, David and Batsheva, Lot's daughters, and dozens of others. God tells us that He is not only our king and judge but our father. We may fail at times and make a mess of things, but as any parent or grandparent knows, to those we have given life there is a bottomless reservoir of love and second chances. And the tradition never fails to remind us that it is God who has given us life.

Four

A Look at the Book
of Ruth

Of the numerous books in the Bible, few are more risqué or more revealing about the Bible's attitude toward sex than the Book of Ruth.

The importance of this particular scroll—one of the five scrolls, or *megillahs,* read in the synagogue over the span of a year—is underscored by the fact that the sages chose Ruth to be read on the exalted holiday of Shavuot, the holiday celebrating Moses' receiving the Torah on Mount Sinai. The Torah is not mentioned in the Book of Ruth, whereas sex is omnipresent; yet the connections abound.

The story begins in a time of cultural chaos. It happened "in the days when the judges were judged." There was famine in the land, literally and spiritually.

A man who lived in Bethlehem—literally meaning "the House of Bread"—journeyed to the nearby land of Moab to find food. The man, Elimelech, came with his wife Naomi and their two sons. Elimelech soon died. His sons married Moabites—one Ruth, the other Orpah. And then the sons died, too. Naomi, hearing that the famine had lifted in Bethlehem, made plans to return.

Naomi and her daughters-in-law set off for the Judean hills. After some contemplation, Naomi told the women they could return to Moab, that they should feel no obligation to stay with her. In her sadness, she wondered whether the in-law relationship she shared with Ruth and Orpah was little more than a civilized sham, a facade that evaporates when the marital link is gone. "Are we really family," she thought. "Were we ever?"

Naomi encouraged her daughters-in-law to find husbands, to get on with their lives. "May God grant," said Naomi, "that you find security, each in the house of [a new] husband. . . . Have I more sons in my womb who could become husbands to you? Turn back, my daughters, go along. For I am too old to have a husband."

Orpah turned back. The Bible tells us that Ruth attached herself to Naomi, using the same word that is used to describe God's command to Adam and Eve to leave their parents and cling to one another. It may be inferred from this that the Bible perceives relationships other than marriages to be special, if not sacred. Sacred relationships between lovers beget special relationships in an ever widening-ripple of others.

Ruth is frequently referred to as "the Moabite," or "Ruth the Moabite." Moabites were descended from Moab, the child of an incestuous affair between Abraham's nephew Lot and one of Lot's daughters. To be a Moabite is to be in disgrace. The Bible in Deuteronomy says that the Israelites were forbidden to marry one of them, or even to accept their conversions to Judaism.

After the destruction of Sodom, Lot's daughter did what she thought she had to do. Living in a warped environment can warp our perceptions. From this act of incest, we got Ruth, David, and the messianic line. As we have seen, morality is sometimes obscure at first glance. Something deserving ostracism for centuries is, centuries later, perceived by sages and mystics to be spiritually transcendent.

Ruth and Naomi returned to Bethlehem. Naomi had another in-law, Boaz, who owned a large farm on the edge of town. Fate drew Ruth to his field and, hungry, she followed the harvesters, gleaning the grain that had fallen. She was a migrant, a drifter, an outcast by virtue of her Moabite heritage.

Boaz saw her from afar and asked a foreman who the stranger is. He was told, "She is a Moabite girl, the one that returned with Naomi from the fields of Moab. She asked to gather the sheaves behind the harvesters."

Boaz told her not to glean in any other field but his. Though she was a Moabite, he has heard of her kindness toward Naomi. And so Ruth gathered his barley and wheat.

Naomi told Ruth to think strategically: "Boaz, our relative, with whose maidens you have been, will be winnowing barley tonight on the threshing floor. Therefore bathe and anoint yourself, dress in your most flattering clothes, and go down to the threshing floor, but don't make yourself known until he has finished eating and drinking. And when he lies down, note the place where he lies down and go over, uncover his feet and lie down. He will tell you what to do."

That night, Boaz ate, drank, and was feeling fine. Ruth went to him as he reclined in the moonlight by the grain pile: "She came stealthily, uncovered his feet and lay down. In the middle of the night, the man was startled, turned, and there was a woman lying at his feet." She said to Boaz, "I am your handmaid, Ruth. Spread your robe over your handmaid, for you are a redeemer," a legal category referring to someone who was permitted to marry her.

The scroll's frequent, almost repetitive, use of the words "to know" and "to lie down" are some of the more obvious sexual euphemisms in the text.

Boaz asked that she "lie down until the morning." So she lay until the morning, arising in the half-light of the predawn, when she could not be recognized. Boaz whispered to her, "Let it be not known that the woman came to the threshing floor." Boaz knew that God understood these matters of the heart better than most people.

Not long after, "Boaz took Ruth and she became his wife, and he came onto her." The witnesses sang out, "May your house be like the house of Peretz whom Tamar bore to Judah, through the offspring which God will give you." On the surface, this is a peculiar blessing, since Tamar had disguised herself as a prostitute to seduce Judah. Yet Tamar and her son Peretz were the ancestors of Boaz. Time literally heals all wounds.

Ruth, meanwhile, shared her joy with Naomi so much that she was almost a surrogate mother for her mother-in-law. Naomi became the baby's nurse. The community rejoiced in the child: "The neighborhood women gave him a name, saying, 'A son is born to Naomi,' and they named the baby Ovade." He grew and had children of his own. One was named Jesse, and Jesse's son was King David.

The town's women said to Naomi, "Blessed be God who has not left you without a redeemer today. May his name be famous in Israel. He will restore your life, sustaining you in old age, for your daughter-in-law, who loves you, has borne him, and she is better to you than seven sons."

The Book of Ruth is a magnificent example of the Bible being a strategic handbook for the sexes, encouraging the woman to initiate sex, even outside marriage, providing that the relationship contains the possibility of fruition, of life, of spirituality. Despite the depths to which anyone may have sunk, despite the stigma of being the child of incest or being a migrant Moabite, the most glorious potential looms within all of us.

For all of the "thou shalt nots" for which the Bible is known, there are dozens of instances in the Biblical canon where we are clearly taught that Judaism is a tradition that appreciates the weaknesses of the heart as much as the stringencies of the law book. Ruth is an example of what David Biale, in his book *Eros and the Jews,* calls "the politics of sexual subversion." Sexual norms spelled out in the Bible are suspended time and again. Indeed, a relationship that fully subscribes to the norm is hard to find in the thousand-plus pages of the Holy Book. And the subversions do not end with the birth of David. The author of the Psalms is revealed to us as someone who steals another man's wife. Yet it is from his relationship with Batsheva, the adulterous woman, that Solomon is born, builder of God's Holy Temple and arguably as great a king as his father, the two greatest heads of state the Israelites have ever known. Perhaps this is because David acknowledged his weaknesses rather than try ex post facto to sanctify them, and because he fully repented after being chastised by Prophet Nathan. As Biale writes, "erotic transgressions are covertly positive. . . . God, it would seem, straddles both sides of the legal fence to advance the fortunes of his chosen people."

And who is chosen? Someone living in the time of Boaz might think that it surely does not include the Moabites, surely it does not include the children of incest or whoring. And yet it does.

The chasidim, many centuries later, developed theories of

sinning that asserted that, based on the Bible itself, no one should feel that love or heavenly sex are elusive because of our imperfections. In messianic times it will be revealed how each of our well-motivated sins were not sins but heavenly chess moves that allowed us to be in a position to further advance God's plan.

We also learn from the story of Ruth that, although God will work overtime to help rectify our weaknesses, there is no room for our passivity. Ruth was the beneficiary of Naomi's strategy, and Boaz—let alone future generations—was the beneficiary of Ruth's seemingly immoral behavior, as she cuddled him in the barn, sharing a blanket in the night.

One of the biggest hurdles in therapy is for the patient to learn how to confront a shattered or tarnished past, the sins of yesterday. This is not to suggest that anything goes, but, as the Book of Ruth teaches, that everything passes, becomes transformed. Dust turns to diamonds, water to wine—this is a tradition as concerned with the forgiven as with the forbidden.

Five

The Sabbath

This chapter will be a romantic guided tour through twenty-five hours of sensual pleasure, based on the Jewish tradition (the Sabbath begins at dusk but ends after dark). As if taking a bite from the Tree of Knowledge, readers will become more aware of their sexiness, the sexiness of religion, and the potential of renewal through the most ancient techniques.

God is the ultimate sex therapist. He/She has created one day a week—the Sabbath, or Shabbos—when God asks, among other things, that we express our love for the Divine by expressing our love for each other. To perfectly follow the guidelines for Shabbos is to have for ourselves a perfectly romantic evening that culminates in love-making, however we like to do it.

One need not be Jewish to appropriate Shabbos for one's own sexual pleasure. But without understanding the inherent sexuality in Shabbos, it is impossible to understand how modest and restrained religious Jews are still able to tap into their highly erotic, otherwise modest selves.

The Sabbath, like all Jewish days, begins on the evening of the previous day, but it does not merely enter when the sun goes down. It is personalized as if it were a bride who is "to arrive." The Sabbath schedule is structured as a weekly wedding for the couple in love. The sages explicitly declared that making love on Friday night is a special blessing. Therefore, almost all of the so-called restrictions surrounding Shabbos are conducive for romance, and virtually everything relating to the Sabbath has a mystical, sexual metaphor.

The Sabbath is about the sanctification and the delight of time, the cessation of earthly preoccupations, a glimmer of the World to Come when the clock ticks at a heavenly pace. We are told to sanctify Shabbat with our heart, soul, and five senses. Says Devarim Rabbah: "Sanctify Shabbat with food and drink, with splendid clothes. Delight yourself with pleasure and God will reward you for this pleasure." In Judaism, God has a male component and a female component. Making love on Friday night is a specific celebration of the unity of God's masculine and feminine aspects.

Shabbos thus commences at Friday dusk with the lighting of two candles, symbolizing, among other things, the male and the female. When Shabbos ends on Saturday night, a braided candle is lit with two candles now entwined, as if in a loving embrace. Almost every custom of the Jewish Sabbath observance facilitates our goal of lighting each other's fire and becoming entwined.

On Sabbath eve, prayers are said to the effect that the lover should find satisfaction within his or her home. Arousal is allowed to take its time, however long that may be. First there are private prayers, introspection. The lovers become attuned to each other, separating from the outside world, from all the pressures of the work week, from the mundane and secondary relationships.

Laws against the use of electricity, engines, batteries, and the like work to the lovers' advantage: walk leisurely, don't drive. Appreciate the beauty of the world, walking under the stars and moon. Knock on the door, don't ring. Don't answer the phone. The television is off. Forget the radio. What may seem like terrible restrictions are really no restrictions at all. It is precisely the ringing phone and blaring television shows that are the real impediments to a good relationship. Forget the CD and tape. The lovers must literally make music together, singing at the table. Romantic melodies called *zemirot*—of queens and angels, of brides and mystery—are sung.

The lovers dine by candlelight. The meal begins with the sharing of wine and loaves of braided challah, an especially rich bread. When they are ready to go to bed, the lovers almost can't help but do so in a highly seductive and seduceable state of mind.

In many hasidic congregations, before the Friday evening prayers are said, while the women are lighting the candles, the men are whispering the words to the Song of Songs, as erotic a book as found in any literature, religious or otherwise. The allegory of the Song of Songs—written by Solomon, husband to seven hundred wives—is that the relationship of God to Israel can only be understood within the liquid dynamics of a male-female relationship, with one partner, then the other, being seductive or elusive.

Listen to the words: "Let me kiss you with the kisses of my lips, for your mouth is sweeter than wine. . . . A garden enclosed is my sister, my bride, a private river, a fountain sealed. . . . How sweet is your love, your perfume more enticing than any spice. . . . Vast floods cannot quench love, nor rivers drown it."

This is quite unlike most other descriptions of the God-human relationship. According to the introduction to the Song of Songs in the Sabbath eve section of the ArtScroll prayerbook (Mesorah Publications), "Solomon foresaw through the Holy Spirit that Israel is destined to suffer a series of exiles and will lament, nostalgically recalling her former status as God's chosen beloved. She will say, 'I will return to my first husband [i.e., to God] for it was better with me then than it is now' [Hosea 2:9]. . . . The prophets," says the commentary,

> frequently likened the relationship between God and Israel to that of a loving husband angered by a straying wife who betrayed him. Solomon composed [his Song of Songs] in the form of that same allegory. It is a passionate dialogue between the husband [God] who still loves his estranged wife [Israel], and the wife, a veritable widow of a living husband, who longs for her husband and seeks to endear herself to him once more, as she recalls her youthful love for him and admits her guilt.
>
> God . . . recalls the kindness of her youth, her beauty, and her skillful deeds for which He loved her so. . . . For she is still His wife, and He her husband, and He will yet return to her.

The reciting of the Song of Songs on the Sabbath eve is based on a kabbalistic teaching—as ArtScroll relates from the classic *siddur, Arugas HaBosem*—that the recitation at this time is powerful enough to save the reader from the suffering of Gehinnom, the Jewish concept of hell.

The midrashic book of Genesis Rabbah teaches that God told the Sabbath Day that the six days of the week have their "mate," but Shabbos will be wed to the Jewish people, Shabbos being the bride. Therefore the kabbalists in the Israeli mountain city of Safad would literally greet the onset of Sabbath like a groom anxious for his bride. At Friday's sunset, after bathing and immersion in the *mikvah* pool, these mystics would dress in white and go out to the fields on the edge of town "to greet her."

One of these kabbalists, Shlomo Halevi Alkabetz, wrote the Lecho Dodi, a haunting song sung in those fields, which begins with the words, "Come my beloved, let us greet the bride." He sings of shedding his anxieties and inhibitions: "Don't be ashamed ... why are you downcast?" Love is coming, sings the kabbalist, heavenly love is coming through the twilight, as the setting sun bathes the singers in the colors of fire and wine.

The Lecho Dodi is followed by readings from the *Zohar,* the major Jewish mystical text, which continues to arouse and remind the Sabbath participants of the joining of male and female later that night. "This is the secret of the Sabbath," says the *Zohar.* "She becomes Sabbath when she becomes united in the secret of Oneness so that God's Oneness may rest upon her. . . . All wrathful dominions and bearers of grievance flee, there is no power but she in all the world. Her face glows with a heavenly light and she takes the holy people below as her crown ... they crown themselves with new souls that come with the Sabbath." Everything is fresh, even our souls.

Although mystical texts have a myriad of meanings, according to Rabbi Aryeh Kaplan, "In ancient kabbalistic texts the word 'Atarah' (crown) also refers to the crown of 'Yesod' (the mystical foundation), or (breaking the kabbalistic code), the glans of the sexual organ. . . . The Atarah is the seat of pleasure." Kaplan explains the liturgical verse, "The righteous man is the foundation of the world," to mean that the Tzaddik holy man who faithfully observes the Sabbath represents Yesod. "Hence, a Tzaddik is someone who can have Divine pleasure. . . . This organ, which is normally associated with the physical, becomes a means of having pleasure from the Divine."

The tradition tells the man and the woman that they are accompanied on this night by angels, greeted in the hymn "Sholom Aleichem":

> Peace upon you, Ministering Angels . . .
> May your coming be for peace . . .
> Bless me for peace,
> May your departure be for peace, Angels of Peace,
> Angels of the Exalted One, from the King
> Who reigns over kings.

If a man is unable to seduce a woman on his own, the tradition virtually whispers in his ear, like a holy Cyrano, the words of Ayshet Chayil, twenty-one verses from the Book of Proverbs, that praise "the woman of valor," a woman who is creative and industrious in business, yet charitable, spiritual, and a source of delight to her family. This song is designated to be sung at the Sabbath evening meal:

> Her husband's heart relies on her . . .
> She repays his good, but never his harm . . .
> She opens her mouth with wisdom, and a
>   lesson in kindness is on her tongue . . .
> Grace is deceiving and beauty is vain,
>   a God-fearing woman—she should be praised.
> Give her the fruits of her hand, and let her
>   be praised at gates by her deeds.

It is only natural, given the mood of Friday night, that some of the verses of Ayshet Chayil have become famous as wedding songs. One bride among the Breslov Hasidim asked her father for a wedding gown, but he was too poor to buy her one. Instead, he put to music the verses of Ayshet Chayil: "Oz V'hadar, strength and majesty are her gown, she laughs looking to the future."

This song is sometimes danced to for hours at Breslov Hasidic weddings, and for the same reason is sung at the "weekly wedding" Friday night, when sexiness is all in the mind and no one has to be rich to have romance.

Many men find poetic language elusive, but want to accept the advice that the man should speak in ways that arouse the woman. Yet they find it somewhat more difficult to actualize the theoretical seduction. Yitzhak Buxbaum, in his compendium *Jewish Spiritual Practices,* reports that a traditional quote might be from Adam, who told Eve, "Bone of my bones and flesh of my flesh, she shall be called Woman." Quoting from Reshit Hochmah, he writes, "See how sweet are these soothing words that Adam spoke to his wife, to show her that they are as one body, and that there is no separation at all between them."

Of course, some women, to be sure, are aroused by rough talk, back-alley language and throw-her-over-your-shoulder sexuality, but there is no evidence of that within the Jewish tradition, which presupposes modesty and feminine delicacy rather than the bawdy. Certainly, though, the disparity between some of the stories in the Bible/Talmud and contemporary religious life suggest that arousal is very much subjective and reflective of time and place rather than any behavioral absolutes. If a woman's or a man's arousal necessitates techniques more associated with honky tonks, so be it, especially if the alternative is an unaroused, uninspired partner.

The tradition's constant is that God is omnipresent and a factor in all relationships, and therefore the sages suggested an arousal technique that is somewhat more celestial than seedy, if that can at all be helped. Buxbaum, in *Jewish Spiritual Practices,* brings advice from the siddur *Yabetz:*

> There is no sexual intercourse without embracing and kissing preceding it. And there are two kinds of kissing: the first is before sexual intercourse, where the purpose of kissing is that the man soothe the woman and arouse the love between them; the other kind is during intercourse itself, where the purpose is to accomplish the two kinds of union, the lower one and the supernal one together.

The act of sex itself is surrounded by ritual and custom, some obscure, some popular. The story that certain religious Jews make love through a hole in the sheet is merely a popular joke among nonreligious Jews who speculate about traditional Jews than it is a fact or requirement. In truth, it would not be allowed because of possible impediment to arousal and pleasure.

Some Hasidim wash their hands before sex, not for the sake of getting rid of dirt, but because sex is perceived as a holy act, and so the hands are washed ceremonially as they are before the Sabbath meal, or before the priestly blessing. In all of these cases, the hands should already have been cleaned with good old soap and water; the ritual washing is simply a symbolic pouring of water over the hands, and it is not presumed to have anything to do with hygiene but has everything to do with holiness.

It is a custom to give charity, even a single coin, to stimulate God's mercy and open our hearts. On Shabbos and holidays when money is not touched, the charity may be specified through intention and fulfilled after the holy day.

The giving of charity also signifies the elevation of the material world into the celestial realms of spirituality, an elevation that the tradition seeks regarding sexuality as well.

The pious learn passages from the sacred literature having to do with sex, or they recite Psalms, such as Psalm 23, which helps negate the negative spiritual forces such as demons, which are as much a part of the Jewish lexicon as are angels. There are theories that demons are created with each seminal emission outside of marital union, as the life force inherent in the semen finds no proper vessel or resting place. According to certain teachers, these demons follow funeral processions, crying out that they are the unborn children of the dead man and they have come for their inheritance.

Reb Nachman of Breslov taught, in his *Likutey Moharan:* "If you believe you can do damage then you can believe that you can repair." He recommends that men say Psalms 16, 32, 41, 42, 59, 77, 90, 105, 137, and 150, each Psalm corresponding to the ten forms of sacred song: Ashrei, Bracha, Maskil, Shir, Nitzuach, Nigun, Tefilah, Hoda'a, Mizmor, and Halleluyah. Each form of song has the power to nullify negative attributes that are prevalent in this world.

Reb Nachman, grandson of the Baal Shem Tov, founder of Hasidic Judaism, said that the recitations of his ten-Psalm remedy releases the spilled seed from the kelipah of evil forces that "captures it." Psalms are the weapons of choice, as the Hebrew word for Psalms—Tehillim—have the numerical equivalent of 485, according to a rabbinic code, which is the identical numerical value of the name Lilith. According to the tradition, Lilith was the primordial female who could have been Adam's mate but chose to escape and become the queen of the demons, charged with instilling sexual fantasies and lures into the minds of young men, who then theoretically seek the wild side of life instead of marital sanctity.

The Psalms also refer to two Divine names and God's attributes of strength and love. According to the mystics, semen contains these Divine attributes, which make it capable of implanting life. The male seed is said to contain the powers of fire and water, heat and liquid, corresponding to strength and love.

Before sex, the Hasidic master known as the Seer of Lublin recommended a meditation to cleave to God beforehand, knowing that during intercourse it is impossible not to become at least momentarily intoxicated with the sheer physical delight. Other masters taught their disciples to give thanks to God for the sublime sensations He gave us as a gift; to instill in the mind that God is not separated from sex—He is the very source.

It is said that Jacob merited being the father of the Twelve Tribes because even during intercourse his mind never lost the connection between God's Supernal Light and sexuality.

The Maggid of Mezeritch taught a pre-sex meditation in which the man imagines himself in the Garden of Eden before the fall, a place without jealousy, anger, or false pride, where everything sensual such as food and sex was delivered with love and delight, where spirituality infused everything and every act freely.

Before sex, some couples pray for the blessing of satisfying one's spouse and/or for having children, if that is possible. As with most prayers in traditional Judaism, the words are phrased in the plural, so the prayer is for all who yearn to have a child or happy unions. Two popular Psalms for these particular thoughts are Psalms 19 and 128. Psalm 19 declares that "night unto night reveals knowledge, there are no words nor language. . . . The sun is like a bridegroom emerging from his chamber, rejoicing like a strong man to run the course, from one end of heaven to the other, and nothing is hidden from his heart. . . . Cleanse me from secret faults, from sins willful or accidental. Then I shall be blameless, innocent of great transgressions."

Psalm 128 speaks of the woman being "a fruitful vine in the very heart of your house. Your children are like olive plants around your table. Thus shall the man be blessed who fears the Lord. . . . May you see the good of Jerusalem all the days of your life. Yes, may you see your children's children, peace be upon Israel."

On Sabbath and holidays, each Grace After Meals is preceded by the singing of Psalm 126: "We were like those who dream. Then our mouths were filled with laughter and our tongues with singing. . . . He who bears his seed, with tears in his eyes, shall return again rejoicing, carrying his sheaves." In the Grace itself is a prayer to be said for your spouse and your seed. Even an unmarried person is advised to say the blessing for spouse and seed, casting a long-distance blessing to wherever the spouse and unborn child might be.

The daytime of Shabbos is no less lusty. The wine is blessed before the lunch meal with a prayer that includes the line, "And the children of Israel shall keep the Sabbath." Nice and dry, say those who think they know Judaism—but what do they know. Rabbi Yakov Emden has shown that the acronym of the Hebrew letters is Bet-Yud-Aleph-Hay—*biyah,* a Hebrew word for intercourse. The most popular Sabbath afternoon activity is a nap—an ideal opportunity to go to bed with your lover in the middle of the day.

The Talmud does not tell a woman when she should make

love. Presumably she is always to be available, as she wishes, except when she is having her period. But men are told exactly how often they should make love, based on their professions.

In the Mishna Ketuvot it is written that if a man is unemployed and has nothing to do, he must make love to his wife at least once a day. A laborer, presumably coming home exhausted, must make love to his wife at least twice a week. A mule driver, often away from home, must make love to his wife at least once a week. A camel driver, traveling vast distances, must make love to his wife at least once every thirty days. Sailors must make love to their wives at least once every six months. That may be because sailors are far from home, or else it may mean that sailors don't need to be reminded. But a newlywed businessman must stay home at least one year. Once again, it shows how wise the talmudists were. If the only purpose of making love was to "be fruitful and multiply" then the Mishna Ketuvot would have said— since the sages were very precise—stay at home until your wife is pregnant. But not so. Rather, the advice given was: stay at home for *one whole year.* Clearly, the sages wanted husband and wife to get to know each other. Getting to know one another is the key to *shalom bayit,* to peace in the home, to building the foundation for a good marriage.

The Talmud tractate on marriage contracts states that the righteous man must make love every Friday night, on the Sabbath. Nevertheless, the sages quickly add that if our lusty righteous scholar wants to have good sex on Sunday, Monday, Tuesday, Wednesday, Thursday, or Saturday night as well, he or she should go right ahead. But only if they have sex with the intention of bringing to it the romantic, mystical uniqueness of the Sabbath. After all, said Rabbi Menachem

Shneerson, the Lubavitcher Rebbe, "From the Sabbath, all the days of the week receive their blessings."

Rabbi Yitzchak Ginsburgh writes, in a pamphlet published with the imprimatur of the Lubavitcher Rebbe, as does Ramban in *Igeret HaKodesh,* that a young Jewish man can learn the secrets of good Sabbath sex from studying Isaiah. Ginsburgh explains that sex is holy when it is done with the intention of bringing a soul into the world, and it says in the *Zohar* that "all Jews are kings." So, how are kings brought into the world? We look in Isaiah and see that Jewish kings were anointed at a slow-running stream outside Jerusalem. Ginsburgh teaches that similarly, when making love, "the husband must be patient," like that slow-running stream, "adjusting his pace to his wife's and waiting for her to climax before doing so himself. By lovingly controlling his own excitement, he spiritualizes the physical act of sex."

Clearly, traditional Jewish modesty applies to the most simple sentences in the Bible. If a single verse in Isaiah about a slow-running stream is then used by Hasidic rabbis to advise us about good sex, imagine what sex tips can be found in the more explicit verses.

The sun begins to set on the Sabbath. A final meal is had, but the songs now are more reflective, almost melancholy about the coming of the ordinary days. One song tells us: "Those who yearn to see the glow, to be part of the union with many-winged angels, rejoice now when there is no anger. Approach me, feel my strength, for there are no harsh judgments."

Given that the Sabbath concludes with the blessings over the braided candle, the light of the fire, and inhaling "the various spices" of life, we can now understand why some Jews say they live from Sabbath to Sabbath. Some of the more mystical sages even attribute the popularity of Saturday night, *the* night of the week to go out with your lover, to the sexual energy released into the world with the end of Sabbath and the blessings over the candles, fire and spice.

Who is to say no, in a world full of mysteries?

Six

Dreaming of Sex

Dreams—at night or in the form of daydreams—are as central to sex as exercise is to an athlete, as weight lifting is to a body builder. The imagination must be superdeveloped. When it comes to sex, the brain must be the most active muscle, straining with ideas and creativity.

When I was a child in Frankfurt, holidays were a time to stretch our imaginations. On the holiest Jewish days, the Kohanim (those men who are descended from Aaron and the priests of the Jerusalem Temple) would give a special blessing to the congregation. The Kohanim would stand shoeless on the platform in front of our synagogue chapel. With white woolen prayer shawls covering their heads and outstretched hands, they looked otherworldly, the holiest of ghosts.

It was considered a most serious misdemeanor for a little girl to have the chutzpa to gaze upon the Kohanim as they were giving the blessing, and I—and all the other children—would hide under the prayer shawls of our fathers and grandfathers (though I must admit that I peeked out from time to time).

As the Kohanim were reciting the Priestly Blessing, alternating with haunting tunes, the congregation would say a key prayer of their own—a prayer not for financial, political, or social success, but a prayer that our dreams be elevated, that our subconscious be purified. The composers of the liturgy advised that when the gates to heaven are wide open, when you have one moment to say a prayer, pray for your dreams.

Imagine saying these words while the Kohanim sing a wordless tune:

> Master of the world, I am Yours and my dreams are Yours. I have dreamed a dream and I don't know what it means. May it be Your will that all my dreams regarding myself and regarding all of Israel be good ones, those that I have dreamed about myself, those I have dreamed about others, and those that others have dreamed about me. . . . If my dreams are good ones, strengthen them like the dreams of Joseph. . . . If they require healing, heal them like Miriam the prophetess from her *tzara'as* [a skin disease].

A word on the stories of Joseph and Miriam is in order. Joseph interpreted Pharaoh's dreams while he was in prison—essentially for the "crime" of not having had sex with Potiphar's wife, who had attempted to seduce him and sought revenge when spurned. Miriam, on the other hand, while wandering with the Israelites in the desert, had her body imprisoned, so to speak, with the disease of *tzara'as* for speculating and challenging Moses about how frequently he had intercourse with his wife. That was none of Miriam's business, and so she was struck with the disease.

The rabbis fully understood that sexuality is a major component of all dreams, daydreams or night dreams, and so they sought to spin gold from straw, to take dreams that at first glance might seem disturbing and turn them into something better.

In ancient days, it was said that there were twenty-four places in Jerusalem for the interpretation of dreams. Of course, says the Talmud, each one of these places gave a different interpretation, but each interpretation was fulfilled—"every dream is in accord with its interpretation."

Rabbi Chisda said, "Every dream is good except that of fasting. . . . Of a bad dream, the worry is sufficient to dissipate it. Of a good dream, the joy is sufficient, but no dream is completely fulfilled."

Nor was any dream completely negated. The rabbis, who took Paradise and prophecy quite seriously, taught that just as intercourse is one-sixtieth of Paradise, a dream is one-sixtieth of prophecy. The sages of the Midrash Rabbah write that "the dream is the unripe fruit of prophecy." The question is, therefore, how do we transform dreams to reality, or even to prophecy?

The Talmud (Brachot) makes a strong case for sex therapy when it claims that if one has a dream that causes anguish, one should go and have it "turned to good." In other words, the dreamer should go to a confidante and work through his or her subconscious and fantasies with someone who understands what the dreamer cannot.

According to Talmudic formula, the dreamer should speak to three friends—the minimum quorum for a court of law capable of passing judgment—who are to start by asking him, "Do not interpretations belong to God? Relate it to me, if you please." No matter what the dream, the dreamer must respond, "I have seen a good dream." The therapists answer: "You have seen a good dream. It is good and may it become good. May the Merciful One transform it to the good. May it be blessed seven times from Heaven that it become good and always be good."

After the dreamer thanks the therapists, "You have changed my lament into dancing for me," the therapists answer with a social blessing: "Then the maiden shall rejoice in a dance, the young men and the old together."

The dreamer is allowed to say, "God, I heard what you made me hear and I was frightened," but the therapist/friend must respond with comfort and encouragement: "Go with joy, eat your bread, and drink your wine with a glad heart, for God has already approved your deeds. And repentance, prayer, and charity remove the decree."

Fantasy and daydreams were encouraged—if within certain boundaries. For example, if a man dreams of having sex with a married woman, the Talmud says that the dreamer still may be assured of a place in Paradise, but only if he does not already know the woman, and has not premeditated about her sexual charms.

While not wishing to encourage adultery, of course, the sages, surprisingly, spend some time empathizing with the dreamers yearning for a married woman. They say, insofar as intercourse is one-sixtieth of the pleasure of Paradise, "surely the more so with a married woman [because] 'Stolen waters are sweeter' " (Proverbs 9:17). "Furthermore, the dreamer is partaking of not only his own portion in Paradise but also the portion of another, which is the case with a married woman who also belongs to another."

A story is told about the power of therapy. A woman once came to Rabbi Eliezer and told him that she dreamed the roof of her house fell in. The rabbi said, "Go home and you will have a son." In other words, go home, have sex with your husband, let him satisfy you. (As we have already learned, when a man brings his wife to an orgasm before his own, that is rewarded by the birth of a son.)

She went home. She had a son. The woman again had the dream that her house collapsed. Rabbi Eliezer repeated his advice: "Go home, have sex, bear a child." She went home, and within a year bore a second son. The woman had the dream a third time, but this time Rabbi Eliezer was not available to counsel her.

The woman was alone in the yeshiva, crying about her recurring dream to the rabbinical students who were, of course, much younger than Rabbi Eliezer and not yet initiated into the advanced skill of Jewish sex therapy and dream interpretation. The rabbinical students heard the woman's dream and told her, "The roof of your home is a metaphor for your husband. He will collapse and you will bury him." Then Rabbi Eliezer returned to the study hall. Hearing what had happened, he admonished the apprentice rabbis, "You killed an innocent man."

He taught them the line from the Torah, "It came to pass as he interpreted for us." In other words, an interpretation can radically affect a situation—resulting in either good sex and a large family, or in tragedy; the choices are that stark. When Rabbi Eliezer told the woman to go home and make a baby, he created a life-enhancing environment in the woman's mind and home in which ill fortune was transformed into a blessing and good luck.

This story also illustrates the importance of picking the right therapist. From the same basic information, one can extrapolate a discussion of sex and babies while another is naturally more literal and not erotic at all, yet the interpretation of either may come true.

One of the most important things to keep in mind about Judaism and sexuality is that most references to sex are a metaphor for spirituality and holy intellectual activity. Likewise, there are also references to Jewish intellectual activity that are a metaphor for sex.

Sometimes the rabbis used this line of thinking to initiate sexual therapy with someone who had fantasies of incest. They would guide the patient to a more acceptable mode of sexual expression, while working to give him greater self-esteem by turning his very disease into a spiritual learning experience. For example, if a man dreams he is having sex with his mother, he might be advised that, aside from the obvious oedipal malfunction, this could be a sign that the man should become actively involved with Torah study. After all, it is written in Proverbs, "Do not forsake the Torah of your mother," Torah often being compared to a woman, a queen, a mother. Further, a dream about having sex with a sister might imply the acquisition of wisdom because it is written, "Say unto wisdom, thou art my sister, and call understanding thy nearest kin, that they may keep you from the immoral woman, the seductress who flatters with her words." Dreams, therefore, are interpreted by matching the dreams' imagery to Biblical passages that employ the same words and references.

When counseling a religious person, said the sages, the intent is not just to put on a Band-Aid, but to help the person realize the power of the mind to cure itself, teaching the religious patient that sexuality is not only healthy but comparable to the most precious things in Judaism: Torah and wisdom. This relieves the religious patient of unproductive, untherapeutic guilt.

The quintessential example of how Judaism seeks to interweave the intellectual and the erotic was the rabbinical debate over whether the highly romantic Song of Songs should be allowed into the Biblical canon. The rabbis interpreted the sexual phrases as referring to the relationship between God and Israel, which elsewhere is compared to husband and wife. Therefore, when it is written in the Song of Songs that a young girl has no breasts, it is said to refer to the Israelites before they were given the two tablets—the two breasts—of the Ten Commandments. The two tablets were said to have spiritually suckled the Children of Israel, giving the new nation what it needed to survive. When one man dreamed of fire shooting out of a woman's breasts, he was referred back to study the Song of Songs and, as the breasts were not his wife's, to the seventh commandment, warning against adultery.

A Hasidic legend tells of a man who had no books save for one single tractate of the Talmud, the tractate Hagigah ("Festival") dealing with the special sacrifices brought to the Temple in the days when sacrifices were an intrinsic part developing the deep intimacy between God and the Jewish people.

So our poor, sweet hasid spends his whole life intimately learning this single tractate inside out, and in the end—whether in a daydream, a spiritual hallucination, or a vision—Hagigah assumes the form of a woman, protecting him as he grows old. After he dies, she is said to walk in front of him, guiding his way into Paradise.

The transformation of holy texts into a loving, erotic object is the rabbinical prescription for a healthy sex life and a healthy spiritual life. There should always be plenty of Heaven in our understanding of sex, and there should always be plenty of sex in our understanding of Heaven. The physical and spiritual manifestations of life are not separate, as they are in some other religious traditions. But they are inseparable, a continuum.

The Baal Shem Tov, founder of the Hasidic movement, had a favorite story about the time Elijah the Prophet went walking through a bustling shtetl marketplace. Elijah was recognized by the local rabbi. The rabbi asked Elijah if there is anyone here who will have a place in the World to Come. Elijah pointed to two brothers who were walking by. "These two," said Elijah.

The rabbi asked the boys what they did. "We are jesters," they said. "If someone is feeling sad, we try to cheer him up. If we see people fighting, we try to make peace."

Gershom Scholem, the founding scholar of Jewish mysticism, explains the story this way: "These jesters are righteous men after the Baal Shem Tov's own heart: They do not sit home thinking about their own salvation, but are working the dirty, bustling marketplace, as the Baal Shem Tov loved to do. The strength of their communion with God is proved in their ability to permeate coarse matter and raise it to the level of spirituality." The most humble and routine activity may then contain the potential for holiness and the supreme transcendent achievement.

For some, sex is considered coarse, or worse than that, routine. However, the Jewish therapist knows that sex is a slice of Paradise, a taste of the World to Come in the here and now. As Elijah teaches, there is no therapy without laughter; there is no Paradise, no sex, as long as someone remains sad, as long as there is fighting. If we can cheer everyone up, if we can bring them closer to Paradise, we are doing God's work, says Elijah.

And that, says the tradition, is the hidden message in every Jewish dream.

Seven

Mikvah

A woman emerges nude from the ocean. In the moonlight, on the beach, her man embraces her, wraps her in a towel, and makes love to her. For twelve days they had only been able to look and speak but not touch. Now, passions unleashed, they could satisfy themselves, each other—and God.

God? Yes. The ultimate threesome for great sex, says this tradition. God, who commanded the abstinence and who originated the idea that the woman immerse and emerge from water under the cover of night before the couple could be reunited after every menstrual cycle.

It is said that to hear a prisoner shoveling under his cell is to know that he is building a tunnel, escaping to freedom. But there were times during the Holocaust, during communism, and during other eras of anti-Semitism that Jews—having nowhere to escape—still shoveled under their homes to build a spiritual escape: a *mikvah*. Even at Masada, where the Jews fought to the last man, woman, and child, archaeologists found that the defenders took the time to build two mikvahs in the fortress, one for the women and one for the men.

According to the rabbis, a town needs a mikvah before it needs a synagogue. But what is a mikvah? A mikvah, the way it is found in most Jewish communities, looks like a miniature swimming pool, with room for perhaps two or three people, and water deep enough to submerge. Often there are stairs leading into the water, and in a man-made mikvah there is always a small hole connecting the pool (filled with regular city water) with a smaller pool that gathers water naturally, from the rain or snow.

The mikvah, whose liquid is restricted to water, must be built into the ground and be nondetachable, excluding items such as a free-standing tub or barrel. The water must come from a natural spring or spring-generated river, or from a sea or lake. If the mikvah is man-made, the water cannot enter it through pipes made of clay, wood, or metal. And the mikvah must contain at least 40 sa'ah, an amount equaling about 200 gallons. Some rabbis have pointed out that one measure of purification is to dilute something with double its volume, and a human body generally displaces 100 gallons or less.

So what does this have to do with sex? Everything. The Torah says, in Leviticus, that "when a woman has a discharge of blood, when blood flows from her body, she shall be a *niddah* for seven days" after the blood has stopped. During this time she may not so much as touch her husband without having immersed herself in a mikvah. This means that lovers must survive at least twelve days a month without sex, including five days commencing with the menstrual flow and at least seven days thereafter. Religious couples sleep in separate beds during this time.

The status of being in *niddah*—one who is removed or separated—is most serious. The Prophet Ezekiel equates touching a woman in niddah to adultery, even if the niddah is your own wife. As it says in Leviticus, "If a man lies with a woman who is a niddah and uncovers her nakedness . . . both of them shall be cut off from their people."

Some have asked, "Why does the Jewish woman have to go to the mikvah to get clean?" But getting clean has nothing to do with it. A woman may only immerse herself there after she is already scrupulously clean—her fingernails, for example, cannot have even the remnant of nail polish when she immerses. There is usually a professional woman who serves as a mikvah attendant whose job it is to assist the women and certify that each woman is thoroughly clean and immerses herself properly.

Women, out of modesty, do not go to the mikvah except in the cover of night. To further enhance modesty, some communities, to house several mikvahs under one roof, construct the building in such a way that perhaps fifty woman could be in private dressing rooms whose doors open into the mikvah so that even the other women never see who else came to the mikvah that night.

Exponents of the mikvah say that when a couple reunites after these twelve days of no-touching, their marriage is renewed. Many Orthodox Jews refer to this as a perpetual second honeymoon. Aryeh Kaplan, whose "Waters of Eden: The Mystery of the Mikvah" is a definitive essay on the subject, paraphrases the Talmud's suggested reasoning: "Unlike many couples, whose sex life becomes almost dull and jaded after a number of years, a husband and wife keeping the rules of niddah experience continual renewal."

Although the rules of mikvah and niddah are almost always expressed regarding a husband and wife, the laws equally regulate the sexual availability of an unmarried woman who may be having her period. It is not uncommon in modern Orthodox circles for unmarried women who are sexually active to go to mikvah once a month, although those who do go often lie about their marital status to the attending mikvah lady, who would no doubt frown on the fact that the young women are having premarital sex.

Although it is not very well known, a mikvah has traditionally been considered more important than the synagogue or any other communal institution. Prayer services, for example, may be held under the sun or the stars, but unless a community lives near a natural mikvah, there is no way of avoiding the necessity of constructing one—immediately, if the community's couples wish to enjoy sexual relations within that first month in a newly built community.

The mikvah is not just used by women. Men have also used a mikvah, usually a separate facility, for spiritual purification. One of the most famous and recommended mikvahs in the world, the Mikvah of the Ari in Israel, is used only by men. That mikvah is a natural water hole, carved out of the rocks, in a cave at the base of a mountain in the mystical town of Safad. There, Rabbi Isaac Luria, known as the Ari, presided over the prime years of kabbalistic study and discovery in the sixteenth century. The mountain springs fill the mikvah with especially icy water that leaves bathers feeling physically as well as spiritually refreshed. This mikvah, because it is in a cave, has the barest of anterooms—a series of hooks on the cave wall on which to hang clothes—and some wooden benches. Most other mikvahs, however, particularly those used by women, are as luxurious, modern, and well maintained as a spa, with fully stocked dressing and preparation rooms, befitting the religious community's regard for the mikvah as a holy experience as well as a place where women prepare for sex after immersion.

Religious men traditionally use the mikvah during the day,

sometimes every day, especially before the Sabbath and on holy days, as well as on the morning after a nocturnal emission. Except for such occurrences, there are no laws that link the men's immersions to sex.

The mikvah is also used as a well of purification that can change the status of an object or person. For example, some Jews will dunk their new dishes and silverware before using them in a kosher kitchen. In the Bible, Aaron and his sons went to "bathe in the waters"—mikvah—before assuming their priestly duties. And a convert must go to the mikvah to conclude the conversion process.

The rabbis say that a convert is like a newborn child. And indeed the mikvah is intended to resemble the birth experience, when a new soul is kept alive in the mother's watery womb before emerging into the world as a new person. Just as a baby enters the world in a state of spiritual purity, a man or a woman may also refine their spirituality, metaphorically to begin life anew with every trip to the mikvah.

Water is one of Judaism's most wondrous things, said to be a person's reconnection to Eden. The Talmud says that all water has its source in rivers cited in Genesis. Water, according to the Bible, was the one thing that existed before creation itself. The Bible says that God "separated the water from the waters," creating sky and seas, but water was always there.

On the afternoon of Rosh HaShanah, the Jewish New Year, Jews traditionally have walked to a flowing river, lake, spring, or ocean to symbolically cast their sins into the purifying waters. And it was with rainwater that God created the flood in Noah's day to purify the earth of its sexual corruption, essentially creating a planet-sized mikvah.

The forty *sa'ah* of water in the mikvah alludes not only to the Great Flood, when it rained for forty days and nights, but to other instances which link forty to a purification process. Moses was on Mount Sinai for forty days and nights, and the Israelites spent forty years in the desert. The Bible and Talmud are loaded with other references to forty as a transcendent number. The spies sent by Moses to explore Canaan took forty days to return. According to the Jewish tradition, forty days is the time it takes for an embryo to humanize. A woman who gives birth is considered ritually excluded for seven days after the birth of a son and thirty-three days after the birth of a daughter, or a total of forty days. Most Biblical references to forty have to do with birth or rebirth.

Kaplan recounts the Mishna's suggestion that the flood lasted forty days because the people of Noah's generation "perverted the embryo that is formed in forty days." Kaplan adds that the *Zohar* gives a similar explanation as to why the punishment for that generation was through water.

> The division of the waters [in the creation story] represents the original concept of sexuality in creation, with the "upper waters" as the male element and the "lower waters" as the female. The generation of the flood perverted this basic concept of sexuality [through homosexuality and bestiality] and therefore the upper waters and lower waters came together to punish them. The Torah thus says, "The springs of the great deep were split open, and the windows of heaven were opened." This same concept applies to mikvah which can be made up of rain waters and spring waters.

The process of birth, the mystery of menstruation, and the opportunities for rebirth and sexual rejuvenation are all inherent in the mikvah process.

But reality and psychology can sometimes intrude. What transpires on the night when the woman comes home from the mikvah can be either glorious or disastrous. Sometimes the P-R-E-S-S-U-R-E of knowing that there must be sex that night might drive the husband to have either a premature ejaculation or an inability to perform. It is well documented that anxiety may be a major component of impotence.

The sages knew that a man is particularly susceptible after twelve days of intensifying sexual abstinence. Premature ejaculation is easily corrected. However, if it is not corrected, the wife does not get sexual satisfaction and, after a while, she is going to develop an avoidance pattern—of either the mikvah or sex, or both.

Sometimes the man will ejaculate too fast because in his anxiety and excitement he will no longer be able to recognize the premonitory sensation—that time before the moment of no return.

Other men may start worrying: "Will I be able to have an erection?" And that one worry is enough for him to lose the erection. Again it's a vicious cycle. He says, "What happened to me tonight will happen to me tomorrow," and then he's in trouble. It will happen again. Sometimes a young religious couple might be naive and inexperienced, precluding the wife's ability to help her husband, physically and emotionally. As with so many aspects of sexuality, one person's erotic renewal is another one's house of horrors. The skillful religious couple learns how to let the period of abstinence and reconnection work for them, as well as in the mysterious ways that it works for God.

The mikvah was so highly regarded in traditional circles that even when King David was about to consummate his illicit relationship with Batsheva he was more concerned with knowing whether she had gone to the mikvah than the fact that she was a married woman. "She came to him and he lay with her, for she was cleansed from her impurity [in the mikvah, following her menstrual cycle], and she returned to her house."

Batsheva conceived from that first union with David, testifying to the wisdom of the sages' arrangement that the woman wait to have sex until her most fertile time of the month.

David sent Uriah, Batsheva's husband, to the front lines of a battle, and Uriah died. Batsheva and David wed. "And the thing that David did was evil in the eyes of the Lord. The Lord sent the Prophet Nathan to David." Nathan told David the following story.

There were two men in one city: one was rich, the other poor. The rich man had many flocks; the poor man, one ewe which he had bought and reared. The ewe grew up together with him, and with his children, and was like a daughter to him. A visitor came to the rich man, who spared his own flock but took the poor man's ewe for his dinner. And David's anger burned greatly against the man, and David said to Nathan, "As the Lord lives, the man that has done this is worthy to die. He must restore the lamb fourfold, because he did this thing and he did it without pity." Then Nathan said to David, "You are that man."

As punishment, and to avenge Uriah, God said:

The sword shall never depart your house, because you have despised Me and have taken the wife of Uriah the Hittite to be your wife. Behold, I will raise up evil against you from out of your own house, and I will take your wives from before your eyes and give them to your neighbor and he will lie with

them in the sight of this sun. For you did it secretly, but I will
do this thing before all Israel and before the sun.

And David said to Nathan, "I have sinned before the
Lord." The prophet told the king, "The Lord has commuted
your sin; you won't die. But because of this deed you blas-
phemed the Lord, the child to be born will die."

The child became sick. David fasted. He prayed "and lay
all night upon the ground." On the seventh day, the baby
died. The servants were afraid to tell David. He saw them
whispering and understood. He asked, "Is the child dead?"
They said, "He is."

David arose from the ground and washed, changed his
clothes, came into the House of the Lord, and bowed down.
Then he came into his own home and asked that bread be set
before him. The king explained: "While the child was yet
alive I fasted and wept, for I said, who can tell? God may be
gracious to me and the child might live. But now that he is
dead, why should I fast? Can I bring him back again?" David
comforted Batsheva, "and went in to her, and lay with her,
and she bore a son, whose name was Solomon."

The story testifies to God's wrath against the abuse of sex
and power, and yet to the ultimate forgiveness. The sages,
searching for deeper understanding, suggested that the forgiveness was for Batsheva's sake, for she went to mikvah and
sought spiritually to purify herself in an impure world, in
impure circumstances. Was she being a hypocrite? Yes, but
so what? ask the sages. When one was a sinner or found a
trend of imperfect behavior, the rabbi-therapists suggested
that the patient limit the damage and recognize good. Impurity breeds impurity and the child died as punishment,
though certainly not every death is a punishment but a fact

of humanity's physical fragility. Nevertheless, impurity is not a permanent stain, and this same couple is capable of giving life to the great Solomon. The parents kept trying, they recognized their faults, repented, and moved on. And every month, for as long as blood flowed from her, Batsheva went to the mikvah, the purifying waters.

There is a proof text that says going to the mikvah was considered to be a higher level even than scholarship, at a time when the highest essence of the Talmudic-rabbinic era was nothing if not scholarship.

Yet in the academy of Elijah the following was taught. Once it happened that a scholar died very young. His wife took his *tefillin* (ritual objects of leather and parchment used by men in daily prayer) and carried them to every study hall, asking why he died so young. And no one could give her an answer. One rabbi said, "I happened to once stop at her house and she told me everything that happened to her. I said, 'My daughter, how did he conduct himself in the days when you were in niddah?' "

She answered, "God forbid."

"And during the days of the week that you wore a *lebunah* [the white garment worn on the days after the period but before going to the mikvah], how was his conduct toward you?"

She answered, "He ate with me, drank with me, and did not refrain from touching me."

The rabbi then said, "Praised be the Holy One who did not spare him for the sake of his scholarship, for as it says [in Leviticus], 'And a woman in the separation of her impurity, you shall not approach.' "

Seemingly harsh, but at the mystical core of classical Jewish family law.

Eight

The Wedding

In traditional Judaism, getting married is not simply a legal ceremony—something that can just as easily be performed in private by a justice of the peace—but a public enactment of Judaism's most sacred communal and familial values.

According to the sages, there is no such thing as coincidence. A man and a woman do not just happen to meet in a bar, at a class, in a bus, or on a cruise, or even through matchmaking friends. Rather, the souls of a husband and wife were united with God's omnipresence before the primal creation: forty days before a child is born it is announced in Heaven who will be his or her mate.

Starting from birth, the angels must work overtime, if necessary, to bring the future spouses together from the opposite ends of the world, if need be, so that they might meet and fall in love.

In the Talmud (Sanhedrin), it is said in the name of Rabbi Yohanan: "Joining couples is as difficult as dividing the Red Sea, they wept first and sang later." A debate ensues. Did not Rabbi Juda say in the name of Rav that "forty days before the embryo is formed a heavenly voice goes forth and announces that this daughter is to be the wife of that son?" The sages explain: The ease of the heavenly announcement has to do with young people falling in love, the romance of youth. The marriage arrangement that is as difficult as splitting the Red Sea refers to the bringing together of older people in second marriages. Rabbi Samuel ben-Nachman said, "For everything there may be an exchange but not for the wife of one's youth."

Some suggest that the effort to fix up just one husband and wife may take centuries, so that the groom's great-grandparents might "be moved" to New York from Cracow, while the angels arrange a migration from Morocco for the ancestors of the bride.

The Talmud, in discussing the laws of the Sabbath, made it clear that on that holy day it is permissible to discuss arranging a wedding for one's child.

There were no limits, it seemed, on the commandment to facilitate a wedding. The rabbis taught that Torah study may be interrupted only for a funeral procession or to lead a bride to her wedding.

The rabbis taught: "He who loves his wife as himself and honors her even more than himself, and he who leads his sons and daughters on the right path and marries them off near the end of puberty's onset, 'You shall know there is peace in your tent.' "

In the Psalms, a man is praised who gives charity constantly. The sages ask, how is it possible to act charitably at all times? The answer is to be a foster parent who raises an orphan until its marriage. If an orphan desires marriage, the sages said the community should rent a house, furnish it, and provide the bride.

Ancient Israel believed that an eclipse of the sun would occur if the community would not come to the assistance of an engaged virgin who complained of poor treatment from her intended.

It is said that after people die, one of the first questions asked of the soul is, "Did you marry?" The Talmud states that "as soon as a man is married his sins stop accusing him." If a man's wife dies, "his advice is no more of use."

An unmarried woman is compared to an unfinished vessel. A bachelor who lives in a large city and does not sexually sin is considered as astounding as a poor person who restores lost items to their owner, or as a rich man who gives charity secretly. But who is to be considered truly rich? Rabbi Akiba said, "He who has a wife that is becoming in all her acts."

There is no overemphasizing the importance of marriage within this tradition. A legend declares that after God created the world, the rest of his time was spent making matches. When destiny's children actually meet, it is popular for friends and relatives to say the marriage is *bashert,* or predestined. An individual maintains the freedom to marry someone who is not predestined, but according to Jewish folklore and rabbinics, this is the sad exception rather than the rule.

The traditional culture endowed each new couple with the belief that the new relationship mattered, not only to the couple but to God and the community. If there were problems, either sexual or social, emotional or economic, psychological or physical, the historic and spiritual impetus of their union led the couple to find a therapeutic solution rather than to call it quits, which would be far easier if the relationship had no transcendent significance and could be canceled without cosmic repercussions. Traditional Jews are taught that while humans are created in the image of God, a man or a woman alone and separate is not the fullest realization of that image. Only together can they fulfill their destiny.

What's love got to do with it? Everything—and nothing. There are two ancient models for how men and women can meet. The Bible tells how Isaac and Rebecca's marriage was arranged by Abraham. On the other hand, the Bible says that "Jacob loved Rachel" and that King Saul's daughter, Michal, loved David, and these loves were a prelude to marriage.

Today, there are still thousands of Orthodox Jews who arrange marriages for their children, basing the match on the religious and cultural similarity of the families. Depending on how traditional the community is, the prospective bride and groom may meet, give their approval, and date in a highly stylized way. The couple will go only to public places, such as hotel lobbies or airport waiting rooms, befitting the laws of modesty, which preclude unmarried couples from being alone in a room. A hotel or an airport is public enough, yet allows the couple to be alone. Rarely, if ever, will the dating couple go to a movie, which is considered a waste of time and too close to being immodest, since so many movies contain sexual situations. Instead, the couple will converse, sharing their dreams, philosophies, and spiritual attitudes. Because these dates are so practical in their orientation, it would be unusual for there to be more than two or three dates before one or the other wants to either move on to someone else or get serious about marriage.

Love is not viewed as a prerequisite but something that will develop naturally when the two mates become family, just as it does between parents and child or between siblings—relationships that are not freely entered into by the participants, either.

While somewhat quaint, the traditionalists say that this

method results in a far lower divorce rate than does marriage American-style. It is a belief borne out by the statistically high number of married couples who "fell in love" or made love prior to the wedding yet divorce—more than 50 percent.

Some "modern" Orthodox communities now have variations of the typical American dating pattern, in which the singles meet independently and are more willing to spend time alone behind closed doors. Even so, these tend to be non-intercourse relationships that involve an extended courtship before the relationship is fully expressed physically.

Ari Goldman, an Orthodox Jew and journalism professor, wrote in *The Search for God at Harvard* that "for many of the Modern Orthodox, sex is not a major area of conflict. Rationalizations abound, including the Jewish teaching that sex is a positive and healthy gift from God. That is, as long as the sex is heterosexual and not adulterous."

Goldman revealed some of the mating patterns at a prominent Orthodox synagogue on Manhattan's Upper West Side.

Once you knew the system it was easy to figure out who was available. In Orthodox synagogues, married men wear the white prayer shawl known as the tallit and married women cover their hair with a hat or a scarf. . . . After the service, the synagogue pours out onto the street. . . . Dating couples join, careful to demonstrate just the appropriate amount of affection in public. Clusters of single people form. Introductions are made, but they are not even necessary because here the easiest pick-up line in New York is at the tip of your tongue: "Shabbat shalom. What did you think of the sermon?" . . . Sex comes later, if at all, in this ritual. And when someone invites you home, it is for a Shabbat meal with a group of friends, not for a roll in bed. At least not initially.

However liberal or classic the dating pattern in the traditional community, when it comes time to get engaged virtually the entire traditional community, modern or not, still observes the custom by which a couple formally asks both sets of parents for their permission and their blessings. This is done more out of respect for parents than respect for the law, since in Jewish law parents are powerless to stop a wedding. In fact, a couple is fully empowered to defy parental objection, as it is written in Genesis that a man is to leave his parents and cling to his spouse.

Although diamond rings are generally considered a popular symbol of an engagement, this custom has no roots in traditional Judaism, which requires a ring only at the wedding itself. In fact, it is the giving of the ring that seals the wedding between a man and a woman, far more than any words or blessings spoken by the rabbi under the canopy. According to the tradition, what counts is that the groom give something valuable that he owns to the bride. In the Sephardic-Oriental Jewish tradition, many grooms give a valuable coin to the bride.

It is a popular Ashkenazi-Western custom to have an engagement reception for the community at which a "Tanayim" agreement is signed stipulating the date of the wedding and other prenuptial specifications. The Tanayim paper may include sentiments such as, "He who finds a wife finds good and finds favor from God who is good, and who says the match is good."

The Tanayim event concludes with a meal, the saying of grace, and sermonettes from elders of the community and scholars. The mothers of the bride and groom break a china plate, symbolizing their half of the deal as well as suggesting that a broken engagement is as hard to repair as a broken plate. Because the Tanayim has legal standing in the traditional community and is recognized as an actual contract, serious problems may ensue if the engagement is broken, almost as serious as a divorce. A trend accelerated in the wake of the Holocaust—when it was not unheard of for a person to sign a Tanayim and then have the spouse "disappear" without a trace—in which mothers would delay the breaking of the plate and the Tanayim ceremony until just moments before the wedding was about to begin. Yet the force of tradition is too strong for it to be done away with entirely as a historical anachronism.

After all, if something is historical it has spiritual weight, for it is a reminder of how generations-past sealed their love, let alone their marriage contracts. And the generations of the past are considered more worthy than that of the present.

Those who still wish to have an engagement ceremony early in the engagement are more likely to have a "Vort" (Yiddish for "word"), at which there is a meal, words of Torah and blessings, and a public assumption of good faith by the two families that they will give the wedding. A Vort, though, is less legally binding than Tanayim. Because even a Vort might give rise to legal problems, many Vorts have become little more than a way for people to get to know the bride or groom at an event with some food, drink, blessings, and sermonettes designed to make the proper impression on friends and family.

Although weddings are the delight of a community, more than one-third of the calendar year is off-limits for such celebrations. A wedding may not be held on any of the fifty-two Sabbaths; the ten days between and including Rosh HaShanah and Yom Kippur; the four fast days, the major Jewish holidays, as well as most of the seven weeks between

Passover and Shavuot; and the three weeks prior to the anniversary of the Temple's destruction on the ninth day of the Hebrew month of Av. Further, there are kabbalistic hints that it is better for a wedding to be held toward the beginning of a month rather than toward the end. Additionally, the bride's menstrual calendar must be consulted, for sex is prohibited during menstruation and for several days after, until the woman immerses herself in the mikvah.

The music at traditional weddings is always Jewish religious music, for, as Rabbi Aryeh Kaplan says, wedding music has "a powerful spiritual effect on the couple's future happiness." The hasidic master, Reb Nachman, taught that the proper music has a therapeutic effect on the couple's future sexual life. This sonic tonic is further enhanced, says Aryeh Kaplan, if the musicians are themselves religious men. It is considered immodest in this tradition for women to play instruments or sing when men are listening. Even the dancing is said to be therapeutic as the bouncing of the body is said to sift away the impurities of the dancer.

Just as the groom gives the bride a ring, it is traditional for the bride to give the groom a *tallis* (prayer shawl). In most Orthodox communities a man only wears a tallis from the time he is married, even though he may have had a bar-mitzvah years before. One reason for this is that a man without a tallis in a sea of tallis-wearing men is being "advertised" to the community as a potential husband.

Another reason is that the tallis is connected by the mystics to sexual temptation, which becomes more of a major concern after marriage than after bar-mitzvah. The command in the Bible to wear the tallis's fringes comes from the Book of Numbers, which states that "they shall be tassels for you and you shall look at them and not be tempted to follow your heart and eyes." The Talmud (Brachot) says that this command is speaking to sexual situations that are forbidden to a married man. There are thirty-two strings on a tallis, thirty-two in Hebrew spells "heart." (In Hebrew, numbers are written with letters, hence rabbis would often utilize mathematics in word interpretation.)

In the traditional Jewish world, a man wears his tallis seven mornings a week, so the message is reinforced daily. In some Orthodox communities, men and women, husbands and wives, are not always buried side by side. But a man is usually buried with the tallis given to him by his wife.

A story is told of a woman who worried that her new groom was not quite as religious as she had hoped. He would go on business trips and leave his tallis at home. She went to the rebbe, who told her that someday her husband will take the longest trip of all, from this world into the next, and the only thing he'll take with him is his tallis. The tallis is an eternal sign of the bond between husband, wife, and God.

In more modern Orthodox circles, where premarital sex is not rare, getting ready for an evening of safe sex requires more than having a condom handy: it requires tallis and tefillin. This has come to be known as "the tefillin date." In other words, the man is so sure he will sleep with his evening's partner that he brings along the ritual objects he will need for his morning prayers.

The communal encouragement and validation for a man about to be married is manifest in the synagogue the week before the wedding, when the bridegroom is called upon to recite the blessings over the Torah. The Talmud notes that a married man will gain a deeper understanding of Judaism's holiest book—a book that, on a mystical level, is so much about sexuality and relationships.

After the groom recites the blessings, following the singing of the Torah verses, the congregation sings a song to the groom and throws bags of candies, so that the new relationship will be a sweet one. Running down the aisles of the synagogue, the little children scoop up the candy even as they are being trained to associate marriage with the highest realms of the Torah and all that is sweet and tasty in this world.

Sometimes nuts are thrown. According to Aryeh Kaplan, the bride is considered a "nut" because she is chaste and closed to all men. Eve, in the Garden of Eden, was referred to as a nut tree in the Blessing of Virgins, which some recite after a marriage is consummated.

In the Song of Songs, the most sexually allusive of all the Biblical canon, one of the lovers says, "I went down to the nut garden." Rabbi Kaplan explains that "before one can enjoy the kernel of a nut, one must first break away the shell. Similarly, before two people can know each other intimately, they must break away the shells that surround them. In marriage, the barriers between husband and wife gradually disappear."

Often, the calling up of the groom to the Torah takes place on the Sabbath one full week before the ceremony, rather than, say, on the Saturday morning before a Saturday night affair. This is sometimes done to allow the bride-to-be to attend the Sabbath festivities, for bride and groom traditionally do not see each other in the week before the wedding so that the wedding night will be one of anticipation and heightened passion. Although it is presumed that the bride and groom have not had sexual relations prior to marriage, this custom of separation is even more useful and cherished among the modern bride and groom who may already have had some sexual interaction. The week of total abstinence—even visual—reinforces the idea that each new relationship comes with a fresh beginning.

It is for this reason that the bride wears white. In the Jewish tradition, the wedding gown is white not to denote virginity but almost the opposite. No matter how sexually promiscuous the bride may have been prior to marriage, the wedding purifies her; she wears white as the color of purity, as fresh as newly fallen snow.

A wedding can fix all that may seem to be broken, such as an indelicate past, healing old wounds and freeing bride and groom from all past transgressions. It is taught that an orphan's dead parents are able to attend the wedding, as are the deceased grandparents, in a noncorporal manner. The ability of the bride, especially while under the wedding canopy, to so bridge the earthly and heavenly worlds has led to the tradition that individuals in need of heavenly favors request the bride to whisper their names as she stands under the *chuppah* canopy.

The small universe beneath the canopy is considered a mini-Eden, the site of the first wedding and a Paradise for the bride and groom to make of as they will. When two people get married, they are deemed to be as sinless as if their bed is in Eden, the fig leaves are thrown over a branch, and "they saw that they were naked and were not ashamed."

Adam and Eve are too often associated with "original sin." Their sin, however, has to do with their eating the forbidden fruit, not their discovery of sex. Their sin of eating the fruit happened *after* they made love. Therefore, their sex in Eden—coming as it did before their forbidden repast— was thoroughly pure and sanctified. In the tradition with which we are concerned, Adam and Eve are more revered for that rapture of sexual bliss than vilified for their serpent-induced transgression. In this tradition, oriented to sexual transcendence, Adam and Eve are models of "original sex"— sex without sin.

To "fix" this sin of the forbidden fruit, the bride and groom have traditionally fasted on the day of their wedding, until after the ceremony. Another reason for the fast is that the wedding day is a mini-Yom Kippur, a Day of Atonement for the bride and groom, an atonement for all that came before and all that will come after. Rabbi Kaplan writes: "Before a person is married, it is very easy to fall into sexual temptation, both in thought and in deed. However, on a person's wedding day . . . the slate is wiped clean. . . . The love that the couple has for one another on their wedding day can annul any misplaced passion that they had in the past," or give eternal dispensation for the future.

Fasting also demonstrates a dominance over physical pleasure. Before entering into a sexual relationship, the bride and groom seek to express their maturity and understanding that sex and other physical pleasures are within their control. No matter how ravenous they may be for either, both sex and eating are postponed until the conclusion of the wedding ceremony.

The Ketubah, or wedding contract, is signed and witnessed before the actual ceremony. It may be written on plain paper, but it has become the custom in many communities for the Ketubah to be a piece of art, elaborate and illuminated, often framed and used to decorate the couple's new home.

The Ketubah begins with the Hebrew letter Bet, as does the Hebrew Torah. Essentially, the Ketubah is a Biblical microcosm; it is dated with a year calculated from the beginning of creation, which is the time of the first sexual rendezvous.

The Ketubah reads:

> On the [day of the week], the [day] of the [Hebrew month] of the [year] after the creation of the world, according to the manner in which we ascribe dates here in [the community of . . .], the groom [mentioned by name] says to this virgin [she is simply considered as pure as a virgin, but that word is one of the few in this document that are replaceable should the couple wish, such as in a second marriage], whose name is [name], daughter of [name]: "Be my wife according to the law of Moses and Israel. I will work, honor, feed, and support you in the custom of Jewish men, who work, honor, feed, and support their wives faithfully. I will give you [money in the event of divorce] which is due you according to Torah law as well as your food, clothing, necessities of life, and conjugal needs, according to the universal custom."

The Ketubah then proceeds to further elaborate the financial obligations. Many sages, however, read into this a couple's sexual obligations as well. The Ketubah's words "work," "honor," and "support" were considered sexual euphemisms for sex far beyond what is simply referred to as "conjugal needs."

After the Ketubah is signed, and sometimes following a brief prayer service in the company of the groom, clarinets and trumpets play a rousing Jewish wedding song that serves as a fanfare while the groom-king is escorted by his male guests and dancing friends to see the bride-queen for the first time in a week. In this ceremony, the bedeken, there is exquisite tension as the two lovers reunite, she in her gown, sitting on a white throne, he arriving to a majestic yet rollicking tune accompanied by what seems like a royal court.

בשלישי בשבת שלשה עשר יום לחרש תשרי

שנת חמשת אלפים ושש מאות וארבעים ושבע
לבריאת עולם למנין שאנו מנין כאן כאמשטרדם איך
ר' מאיר ———— בן ר ———— בי אל ———— הו
אמר להלהדא בתולתא מרים ברת ר ———— בי חיים
הוי לי לאנתו כדת משה וישראל ואנא אפלח ואוקיר ואיזון
ואפרנס יתיכי כהלכות גוברין יהודאין דפלחין ומוקרין
וזנין ומפרנסין לנשיהון בקושטא ויהיבנא ליכי מהר בתוליכי
כסף זוזי מאתן דחזי ליכי מדאוריתא ומזוניכי וכסותיכי
וסיפוקיכי ומיעל לותיכי כאורח כל ארעא וצביאת מרת
מ ———— ים בתולתא דא והות ליה לאנתו ודין נדוניא
דהנעלת ליה מבי נשא בין בכסף בין בדהב בין בתכשיטין
במאני לבושא ובשמושא דערסא חמשין לטרין וצבי
ר ———— בי מאיר ———— חתן דנן והוסיף לה מן דיליה
חמשין לטרין סך הכל מאה לטרין דכסף וכך אמר
ר ———— בי מאיר ———— חתן דנן אחריות שטר
כתובתא דא ותוספתא דין קבלית עלי ועל ירתי בתראי
להתפרע מכל שפר ארג נכסין וקנינין דאית לי תחות כל
שמיא דקנאי ורעתיד אנא למקני נכסין דאית להון אחריות
ודלית להון אחריות כלהון יהון אחראין וערבאין לפרוע
מנהון שטר כתובתא דא ותוספתא דין ואפילו מן גלימא
דעל כתפאי בחיים ובמות מן יומא דנן ולעלם ואחריות
שטר כתובתא דא ותוספתא דין קבל עליו ר ———— בי
מאיר ———— חתן דנן כחומר כל שטרי כתובות ותוספתות דנהגין
בבנת ישראל העשוין כתיקון חכמינו ז"ל דלא כאסמכתא
ודלא כטופסי דשטרי וקנינא מן ר ———— בי מאיר ————
בן רבי אליהו חתן דנן למרת מ ———— ים
ברת ר ———— בי חיים בתולתא דא בכל מה דכתב
ומפורש לעיל במנא דכשר למקניא ביה הכל שריר וקים

יצחק חיים ————

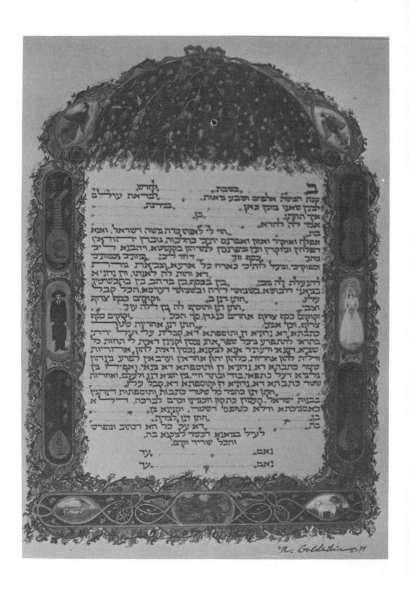

N. Goldstein 1919

Three *ketubahs,* spanning almost three centuries. The first is from Livorno, Italy, and dates to 1782. A large inscription appears in Italian: *SERBIÁN FELICITÁ SI DOLCI PATTI,* which translates to "May these sweet terms serve happiness." #34.57. Parchment, ink. The second stems from Amsterdam, circa 1886. Written in standard Ashkenazi text, the ketubbah reveals two heraldic nude *putti,* standing behind inscribed shields and trumpeting the verse from Jeremiah 33:11a: "The sound of mirth and gladness." #34.280. Paper, printed (added later: watercolor). The final ketubbah is a contemporary one, from Minnesota in 1979. Framing the text is a highly ornamental *chuppah* scene in a vineyard setting. In the borders we find the bride, dressed in white, with flowers in her hands, and the groom, decked out in traditional black hassidic garb. Each picture is set in an oval gilt frame inscribed in black with verses from the Song of Songs: "Ah, you are fair, my darling, ah, you are fair, with your dove-like eyes" (1:15)—for the bride; and "Like an apple tree among trees of the forest, so is my beloved among the youths. I delight to sit in his shade, and his fruit is sweet to my mouth" (2:3)—for the groom. #34.265. Paper, watercolor, acrylic, gold paint, ink; artist and calligrapher: A. Nancy Goldstein. (All three ketubbahs courtesy of the collection of the Hebrew Union College Skirball Museum. Photography by Lelo Carter.)

The groom approaches the bride, their eyes lock, and he lowers her veil over her face, as the Biblical Rebecca lowered her veil before meeting Isaac. (Because Abraham and Sara were married before we are introduced to them in the Bible, it is Rebecca who is considered the first bride in the long unbroken tradition of Jewish weddings.)

There are other reasons for the veiling: to perform an act of modesty after the bride, on her day of greatest beauty, has received guests and a myriad of praise; to show that the groom is not as interested in the external physical beauty as in the bride's internal spiritual beauty that is veiled by her corporal appearance; to recall the blind faith of the Israelites as they—the bride—followed God, the metaphorical groom, out of Egypt and into a decades-long journey into the unknown, over the desert and fields of stone.

In some traditions, the bride is then blessed by the onlookers in the same words as Rebecca was blessed before marrying Isaac, and as girls are blessed every Sabbath eve: "Our sister, may you become thousands. . . . May God make you like Sara, Rebecca, Rachel, and Leah." Frequently the groom is blessed as well.

It is the highest honor and obligation to dance with the bride or groom. Rabbi Chelbo, in the name of Rav Huna, said: "He who does not cheer the bridegroom . . . transgresses against the Five Voices" (in Jeremiah where it is mentioned, the voice of gladness, the voice of joy, the voice of the bridegroom, the voice of the bride, the voice of those who say, praise Ye, the Lord of Hosts). And if he does cheer the groom, what will be his reward? Rabbi Simon ben-Lakish said, "He will merit the Torah." Rabbi Abuhu said, "To cheer the bridegroom is considered as meritorious as if he brought a thanksgiving offering." Rabbi Nachman ben-Isaac said, "It is as if he had rebuilt the ruins of Jerusalem."

The groom precedes the bride down the aisle, as Adam was in the Garden before God brought Eve to him, just as God was the first one at Sinai before the Israelites arrived. No, the groom is not God, of course, but weddings are intended to reverberate with historical and theological imagery so as to lend gravity and eternity to the occasion.

Just as the angels Gabriel and Michael escorted Adam to his wedding canopy, the groom is escorted as well, usually by his parents. As he passes down the aisle, the guests rise row by row, as if in the presence of royalty. The guests sit again when the groom passes. This act of respect is repeated for the bride.

Those escorting the bride and groom usually do so while holding two braided candles, one for each escort. The candles evoke a serene beauty, their braids suggesting the intertwining of male and female, their heat the heat of passion, their fire a warning that if the marriage loses its spiritual dimension it is in danger of inflicting the pain of flames.

When the groom arrives under the chuppah canopy, according to one custom, he is helped into a *kittle,* a white cotton or linen robe without pockets, symbolizing not only the groom's purity but the shroud into which he will be helped after death. This is not as morbid as it seems, for the dead are believed to ascend to a holy and higher world, an Eden of the afterworld. Some rabbis maintain that it is the idea of death, and meeting one's maker, that keeps a spouse honest.

The chuppah itself is another demonstration of the unity of bride and groom. It is comprised of a large tallis or other cloth, held high by four poles over the bride and groom, symbolizing the roof and four pillars of their home. The chuppah is open-sided, a reminder of the tents of Abraham that were open to all, from all four corners of the world.

In some communities a tallis is draped over the couple, one of the signs to the public that the couple is united within a household.

When the bride arrives under the chuppah she circles the groom seven times, or three times, depending on custom. Just as the groom is giving the bride a ring of metal, she is creating a ring of the spiritual within which she will enclose and enrapture him. Some mystics also assert the bride's circling the groom is evocative of the vaginal embrace of the penis, though modesty has relegated that interpretation to the dusty shelves.

Seven and three are the most mystical numbers, each evoking dozens of holy images such as the seven days of creation that culminated in the creation of woman, and the new love is a symbolic re-creation of the world. Three, among other things, is thought to mirror God's promise to the Israelites that "I will betroth you to me forever. I will betroth you to me with righteousness, justice, kindness, and mercy. I will betroth you to me with faith, and you will know God." That last quotation, from the Book of Hosea, is recited on every morning that Jewish men put on their tefillin, its leather straps and boxes containing holy scripture, worn during prayer.

The chuppah concludes with the recitation of the Seven Blessings, which thematically build from the beginning of creation to the climax of this marriage and the messianic potential within all married love.

The blessings, as follows, are said while holding a cup of wine:

1. Blessed are You, Adonai our Lord, King of the universe, creator of the fruit of the vine.

2. Blessed are You . . . who created all things for his glory.

3. Blessed are You . . . creator of man [Adam].

4. Blessed are You who created man in his image, in the image of his plan, who prepared for him an eternal structure, blessed are You God, who fashioned the man.

5. Bring intense joy and celebration to the barren one through the ingathering of her children surrounding her in gladness, blessed are You who gladdens Zion through her children.

6. Gladden these beloved companions as you gladdened your creature in the Garden of Eden in the beginning of time, blessed are You who gladdens groom and bride.

7. Blessed are You, Adonai our God, king of the universe, who created joy and gladness, groom and bride, mirth, happy song, pleasure, delight, love, brotherhood, peace, and companionship. Adonai our God, let there soon be heard in the cities of Judah and the streets of Jerusalem the sound of joy and the sound of gladness, the voice of the groom and the voice of the bride, the sound of the grooms jubilant from under their chuppahs, and of the young from their song-filled feasts; blessed are you who gladdens the groom with the bride.

Note that in the sixth blessing we speak of the groom and the bride, and in the seventh of the groom with the bride. The tradition is cognizant of the reality that at times the lovers are separate individuals and at other times they are a singular unit. Part of the blessing is that they have the wisdom to know when to let the other have autonomy and independence—then will come the blessing of groom with the bride. Although they are now one family, they still deserve and require individual blessings.

The blessings correspond to the blessings God gave Adam and Eve in Eden—to be fruitful, multiply, fill the world, conquer it, and dominate the fish, birds, and animals. All of nature was their gift.

These Seven Blessings are recited throughout the first week of marriage. Instead of going off on a honeymoon, the couple is entertained at a series of mini-wedding feasts for the next seven days.

Under the chuppah, the Seven Blessings signify the actual ceremony's conclusion, marked by the breaking of a glass that is wrapped in a cloth. The reasons for this are many. The most frequently cited is that even at times of greatest joy the lovers must remember that the world is in an incomplete state, symbolized by the destruction of the Holy Temple in Jerusalem and the new couple must assume, among their marital duties, a commitment to rectify the world's imperfections. Other reasons include commemorating the breaking of the Ten Commandments; evoking our mortality; or giving Satan his five seconds in the sun, so as not to arouse the Evil Eye with so much joy and happiness.

The sages picked glass, however, as the material to be broken because it—like us—is easily shattered but easily molten and reformed, reconstructed in essence in its original purity.

Rabbi Shlomo Carlebach asks: "Why don't I break a glass every day and not just under the chuppah? The answer is like this: If I am homeless and live on the subway and someone tells me their house falls down, how much does it hurt me? Not much. But when you are standing under the chuppah, and God gives you a house, suddenly you become aware of the sadness that God has no house."

Says Rabbi Carlebach:

> We break a glass to remember Jerusalem. Do you know how much pain we went through for two thousand years to fix Jerusalem, from the day the Romans burned it until 1967 when Jews once again had access to the whole city? So much, right? So you know what the groom says to his bride right before they leave the chuppah? He says, if God forbid anything gets broken between us, I'm ready to go through that much pain in order to rebuild our home again.
>
> As long as you don't have your soulmate, you're not strong enough to fix the world. When you have a soulmate and a home you can fix the world. So when you leave the chuppah, you say "Master of the World, I'm ready. Send all the broken glass to me."

After the glass is broken under the chuppah, everyone shouts "Mazel Tov!"—but not in Jerusalem. There, where the Temple actually stood, one has the feeling that people should not be shouting "Mazel Tov!" at a moment that recalls national tragedy. So, according to some in Jerusalem, the glass is broken earlier in the ceremony and the cheers come after the seventh blessing.

After the ceremony comes the couple's seclusion behind closed doors, a privilege of marriage. This seclusion, called Yichud, recognizes that a marriage whose walls are always open like a chuppah is doomed to failure. There must be a time, the bride and groom are told, when they are alone. Indeed, the folk tradition says that there is no greater blessing for new lovers than the wisdom to know when to open their doors and when to close them.

Rabbi Chanina ben-Raba said: "Everybody knows why the bride enters the nuptial chamber. Yet he who speaks about it with profane language [will dispel] even a Divine decree granting him seventy years of happiness—such a decree will be changed to evil against him."

The wedding meal at traditional weddings is startling because of two customs. One, there are several tables set aside for the community's poor, for students, the elderly or down-and-out who could use a good meal and whose fortunes might soar in the glow of the bride and groom. And the bride and groom are able to be blessed by launching their first moments as a couple with acts of charity and kindness.

Another custom is gender-segregated dancing. The idea behind this is that the focus of the partying should be on the bride and groom, not on whether you have a date or not. The separate dancing also ensures that everyone is able to participate in the gaiety, even if they came alone. Some of the dances, however, are quite sexually charged, even if segregated. A more legal reason is that the sages deem it immodest for men and women to dance together in public.

Just as the Sabbath is intended to provoke spiritual contemplation and not merely consist of the simple deprivation of, say, watching television, so too a wedding is supposed to be more about the prayers flowing to and from the chuppah and the couple than it is to be about the ceremonial site becoming the town disco. A wedding should revolve around intimacy.

A wedding is supposed to be about small-scale messianism. A lover, like the Messiah, has the power to take everything wrong and make it right again. Rabbi Carlebach teaches that we keep waiting for the Messiah to save the world, but sometimes we have the privilege to act as a messiah for one another. That, in the ideal, is marriage.

How should a bride be praised when one dances before her? The sages debate. Bet Shammai says, "Describe her as she is." Bet Hillel says, "Call her a handsome, graceful bride." It was asked of Bet Hillel, "Suppose the bride is lame or blind, should we still sing as you say?"

Bet Hillel suggested that one should not point out her flaws to the groom or to the Creator of all brides. And so Bet Hillel sang of the beauty inherent in all brides.

When Rav Dimi came to Babylon from Israel, he said, "This is the way they sing before a bride in Israel: 'She has neither paint nor nail polish nor hair dye—yet she is graceful as a gazelle.' "

Rav Acha would put the bride on his shoulders and dance with her. When the rabbis asked him, "May we do the same?" He answered, "If the bride is like a beam on your shoulder and you will not get aroused to impure thoughts, then you may. But not otherwise."

Rabbi Judah bar-Ilai would dance with a myrtle branch before a bride, singing, "A handsome and graceful bride." Rav Shmuel bar-Isaac would dance with three myrtle branches. Seeing this, Rav Zera said, "The old man is an embarrassment." But when he (the old man) died, a column of fire was interposed between him and the rest of the world—which occurs only once or twice in a generation. Rav Zera then said, "The myrtle branch he was using to dance before the bride must have been a blessing to him."

The holiday of Tu B'Av was the ancient day for social daring. According to Rabban Shimon ben-Gamliel, Israel had no days as festive as the fifteenth day of the month of Av (Tu

B'Av) and Yom Kippur. On Yom Kippur, all sins are forgiven. On Tu B'Av, the young ladies of Jerusalem would step out in white dresses, all of which were borrowed, so that those who had none would not be embarrassed. Rich girls were forbidden to wear their own clothing. All the dresses required immersion in a mikvah. The girls would go out and dance in the vineyards. And what would they sing? The pretty girls would sing, "Young man, lift up your eyes and see what you are choosing for yourself," as a wife is primarily for beauty and her potential as a sex partner.

Maidens who were not particularly attractive but came from honorable families would sing, "Do not pay attention to beauty. Pay attention to family," as a wife is primarily for childbearing and creating a family.

Those who were plain and from undistinguished families would sing a verse from the Book of Proverbs stressing inner majesty, "Grace is deceptive and beauty is vain, a woman who fears God should be praised," but only with the provision that after marriage they be adorned with gold, jewelry, and beautiful clothing as that can compensate for a lack of natural beauty.

Rabban Shimon ben-Gamliel explained a related verse: "Go forth and gaze, O daughters of Zion, upon King Solomon, adorned with the crown his mother made him on the day of his wedding and on the day of his heart's joy." This is an allegory, the king being God, the mother being Israel, the wedding being the day the Torah was given on Sinai, the crown being the Holy Temple: "May it be rebuilt speedily in our day."

Why the fifteenth of Av? Rav Yehuda, in the name of Shmuel, explains that was the first day in which the Twelve

Tribes were able to marry outside their own tribes. Until then, Israelites were restricted to their native tribes for partners in romance. On that day, young women would dance in the vineyards. Men who lacked a wife would go there to find one. Even those who were older and no longer married were urged to remarry. The sages said, "Although a man has many children he is nevertheless prohibited from remaining single" (in the event of his wife's death or divorce). Rabbi Joshua added that a man should try to have children even when he is old.

It was hoped that all would sleep with their spouses in a marital bed like that of King David, where a harp hung over the headboard. At midnight a northerly wind would blow in upon the strings of the harp, causing it to play the most beautiful melodies.

As Samuel said to Rabbi Juda, "Scholar, take and eat; take and drink; the world we are to leave is like a wedding banquet that goes by all too quickly."

Epilogue

People have always asked me, especially when I first started out in the media, how I was able to break through so many barriers when it came to talking about sex. My usual answer has been to list the possible reasons: my education, particularly my training as a sex therapist; my age, which made my speaking so openly about sex less threatening; and my accent, which reminded people of Freud and also gave a foreign flavor to the frank sexual terms I always use, perhaps making them more acceptable.

My upbringing as an Orthodox Jew gave me a solid foundation in a moral tradition that comes across to my listeners and readers, even when I am talking about orgasms or different positions. And the fact that Jews don't look upon sex as a sin, but rather as a pleasurable duty, made it easier for me to talk about it without embarrassment, which in turn made it a more comfortable experience for my audience.

Also in the Jewish tradition is the concept that if only the mother or the newborn can be saved, it is the mother's life that comes first. This made it easier for me to take a stand in favor of abortion, though never as a method of contraception, but only as an extraordinary measure.

The Jewish tradition also places importance on peace in the home—*shalom bayit*—and since sexual pleasure is an integral part of that process, to me it was a *bracha* (blessing) and a *mitzvah* (a positive commandment) to help couples with this important aspect of their relationship, rather than something I should be ashamed of doing.

By espousing this concept of Heavenly Sex, not only for Jews but for all people, I have tried to help better the sex life of those who hear my advice. So while Heavenly Sex may not be feasible all the time, it is something that I wish for my readers as often as is possible for them. And may they thank their God when it occurs.

Appendix One

Legal Codification

In the Oral Law tractate of Makkos, Rabbi Simlai taught that "613 commandments were related to Moses, 365 prohibitions corresponding to the days of the solar year, and 248 positive initiatives corresponding to the parts of the human body."

An extensive literature evolved over the millennia as to where in the Torah these 613 are enumerated. The Bible itself does not differentiate legend from law on the theory that every letter in the Bible is of mystical import, with a galaxy of lessons, and no letter is more important than another. Nevertheless, befitting the idea that each of the commandments relates to "the parts of the body" under the sun, there are a vast number of laws governing sex and relationships.

These 613 commandments serve as the constitution for rabbinic law, insofar as all subsequent laws are required to show their origin, or answer for derivation, from these core doctrinal passages. The following are sixty-five of these commandments that seem to reflect Judaism's and monotheism's earliest understanding of sexual laws and values.

The first set of square brackets encloses the Biblical verses from Genesis, Exodus, Leviticus, Numbers, and Deuteronomy from which the laws are derived. A second set of brackets refers to the Oral Law, the Babylonian Talmud's tractate and folio or chapter numbers in which the commandments are debated, or simply where they are illuminated through stories and esoteric commentary.

A tractate listed without a number indicates that virtually the entire tractate deals with the topic. As the style of the Talmud is one more of free association than a scientific or academic volume, a topic may be touched upon in several tractates. Any indexing of talmudic subjects is inherently inexact, as the Oral Law, unlike the Bible, is literally written in free association, with virtually no punctuation marks to delineate individual verses.

Readers seeking to look up these passages should be aware that there are slight variations between the Hebrew and Christian systems of Biblical chapter-and-verse, with the debate extending even to differences about the phraseology of basic things such as the Ten Commandments. For example, although both Hebrew and Christian scholars place the Ten Commandments in Exodus 20 and Deuteronomy 5, the Hebrew Bible subdivides the Ten Commandments into fourteen sentences in Exodus (the first broken tablets) and into twelve sentences in Deuteronomy (the second tablets); the Christian canon punctuates the exact same commandments into seventeen and sixteen verses, respectively. There is further disagreement as to how the commandments are to be numbered, although there is no dispute over the original, unpunctuated words.

It is hoped that the verses listed below are only a starting point that will inspire readers to open their Bible of choice and to examine the spiritual and narrative context in which these commandments were given.

Commandment 1

To create family, to marry and have children [Gen. 1:27–28; 2:18, 2:24–25] [Yevumos 61]. "Male and female he created them. God blessed them and said to them, 'Be fruitful and increase.' . . . It is not good that man should be alone. . . . Hence a man leaves his father and mother and clings to his wife and they shall become one flesh. The two of them were naked, the man and his wife, yet they felt no shame."

This law is applicable only to men over age 18. If after ten years the wife does not conceive, the husband has the option of taking a second wife to fulfill this commandment.

Traditionally, "abortion on demand" has been interpreted as a violation of the command to be fruitful and multiply. Rabbis, however, have always permitted abortion when necessary for the woman's medical or psychological well-being, but not as contraception and not as "choice." This allowance for necessity has been freely adapted by Judaism's more liberal wing to coincide with modern American law, but it is interpreted far more narrowly—almost to the point of nonexistence—by the classic Orthodox. Moving to the right along the Orthodox spectrum, abortion is not a matter of "choice" but reserved only for women whose circumstances are truly dire; exhaustion or family planning is not considered a legitimate enough reason. In hassidic and yeshiva circles, abortion is rare, almost stigmatized, and not allowed for controlling the baby's sex or avoiding most birth defects. It is even less debated than in the most traditional U.S. Roman Catholic communities.

Commandment 2

Males must be circumcised on the eighth day of life, health permitting [Gen. 17:10] [Shabbos 19].

Of the 248 positive commandments, this and the Passover sacrifice [Ex. 12:6] are the only two whose violation was deemed worthy of punishment by excommunication. "Such shall be the covenant between Me and you and your offspring to follow which you shall keep: every male among you shall be circumcised."

Commandment 3

"You shall not commit adultery" [Ex. 20:13] [Sanhedrin 84; Kesubos 44]. Rabbinical law amended this seventh of the Ten Commandments with a vast number of laws pertaining to sexual modesty, such as the prohibition of men and women being alone together, except if they are immediate family. Adultery with a married woman was one of six capital crimes, punishable by strangulation, and the only capital crime that has to do with human sexuality.

Adultery is the only one of the Bible's sexual laws that was considered applicable to all humanity. The Oral Law recognized "The Seven Laws of the Sons of Noah," conformity to which earns any person a "share in the World to Come." (The seven laws are: the obligation to establish or accept a system of administering justice; prohibitions against murder, adultery, idolatry, theft, cursing God, and eating anything that was severed from a living animal.)

Commandment 4

"You shall not covet your neighbor's wife" [Ex. 20:14] [Baba Metzia 5]. This, a part of the Ten Commandments' final injunction, is one of the few sexual laws that involves intent rather than action.

Commandment 5

When slavery was legal, a man could not purchase a Jewish girl without marrying her, or his son marrying her [Ex. 21:8] [Kiddushin 18]. "If she [a servant girl] proves to be displeasing to her master, who designated her for himself, he must let her be redeemed; he shall not have the right to sell her to outsiders since he broke faith with her." Marriage was assumed in the original transaction with the girl's father, as it was inconceivable that even a slave girl should remain outside a sexual relationship that recognized her rights, and her servitude might preclude her prospects.

Commandment 6

A subdivision of the previous law; once a master enters into a sexual relationship with a servant, he must provide for her as a transition toward her freedom [Ex. 21:9–10] [Kiddushin 19]. "And if he designated her for his son, he shall deal with her as is the practice of free maidens. If he marries another, he must not withhold from this one her food, her clothing, or her conjugal rights."

Commandment 7

"If he fails her in these three ways, she shall go free, without payment." What is accepted in the society as a fine standard of food, clothing, and sexual relations is established as a husband's responsibilities toward his wife [Ex. 21:11] [Kesubos 47]. Even a servant taken as a lover by her master assumes all the sexual and social comforts the Bible recognizes as a marital requisite.

Commandment 8

"When men fight and one of them pushes a pregnant woman and a miscarriage results, but no other damage ensues, the one responsible shall be fined according as the woman's husband may exact from him, the payment to be based as the judges determine. But if other damage ensues, the penalty shall be life for life, eye for eye, tooth for tooth, hand for hand, burn for burn, wound for wound, bruise for bruise" [Ex. 21:22–25] [Baba Kamma].

This passage indicates that the Torah did not see the fetus as a complete human prior to actual birth, otherwise "life for life" would come into play for a miscarriage. Nevertheless, it does indicate that the fetus is not spiritually worthless and, if miscarried, the parents indeed suffer a loss and deserve compensation. The Jewish laws of abortion are a mediation between this passage and the first commandment in this listing.

Commandment 9

"If a man seduces a virgin for whom the bride-price has not been paid, and lies with her, he must make her his wife by payment of a bride-price [dowry]. If her father refuses to give her to him, he must still weigh out silver equal in accordance to the bride-price for virgins" [Ex. 22:15–16] [Kesubos, chaps. 3–4].

Commandment 10

"When a man has an emission of semen [outside of intercourse], he shall bathe his whole body in water [a mikvah] and remain [ritually] unclean until evening. All cloth or leather on which semen falls shall be washed in water and remain unclean until evening. And if a man had carnal relations with a woman, they shall bathe in water and remain unclean until evening" [Lev. 15:13–18] [Shabbos 86].

The "and if" shows that the Torah presumed that not all sexuality would be within marital intercourse, but there were laws for these sexual situations as well. An example today may be found among the more modern Orthodox who still value virginity but who engage in virtually all other nonintercoursal activity. Rather than wrestle with the difficulties of sexual abstinence, there is an ethic of safe sex known as "everything but," which can very well possibly lead to a seminal orgasm. In this situation the above commandment applies and the laws of mikvah are observed.

Commandment 11

"When a woman has a discharge, her discharge being blood from her body, she shall remain in her impurity seven days; whoever touches her shall be unclean until evening. Anything that she lies on during her impurity shall be unclean, and anything that she sits on shall be unclean. Anyone who touches her bedding shall wash his clothes, bathe in water, and remain unclean until evening. . . . And if a man lies with her, her impurity is communicated to him; he shall be unclean seven days, and any bedding on which he lies shall become unclean." Laws of menstruation continue for the rest of the chapter. In recognition of this commandment, most Orthodox couples sleep in separate beds, or in single beds placed side by side but technically of different bedding [Lev. 15:19–33] [Nidda].

Commandment 12

"None of you shall come near anyone of his own flesh to uncover nakedness; I am the Lord" [Lev. 18:6] [Shabbos 13, 64; Kiddushin 70; Yevumos 62; Nidda 13].

Commandment 13

One may not "uncover your father's nakedness" [Lev. 18:7] [Sanhedrin 54].

Commandment 14

One may not "uncover your mother's nakedness" [Lev. 18:7].

Commandment 15

One may not uncover "the nakedness of your father's wife" [a stepmother], even after the father dies [Lev. 18:8].

Commandment 16

It is forbidden for a man to have relations with his sister or half-sister [Lev. 18:9].

Commandment 17

... with one's granddaughter from a son [Lev. 18:10].

Commandment 18

... with one's granddaughter from a daughter [Lev. 18:10].

Commandment 19

... with one's daughter [Lev. 18:10].

Commandment 20

... with a half-sister from the father's side [Lev. 18:11].

Commandment 21

... with one's father's sister or half-sister [Lev. 18:12].

Commandment 22

... with one's mother's sister [Lev. 18:13].

Commandment 23

One may not enter into sexual perversions with one's uncle [Lev. 18:14].

Commandment 24

One may not have sexual relations with one's father's brother's wife [Lev. 18:14]. Rabbis amended this to include one's mother's brother's wife.

Commandment 25

One may not have sex with a daughter-in-law [Lev. 18:15].

Commandment 26

One may not have sex with one's brother's wife [Lev. 18:16].

Commandment 27

One may not marry a woman and her daughter [Lev. 18:17].

Commandment 28

One may not marry a woman and her son's daughter [Lev. 18:17].

Commandment 29

One may not have sex with a woman and her daughter's daughter [Lev. 18:17].

Commandment 30

One may not marry two sisters [Lev. 18:18]. Jacob married two sisters, Rachel and Leah, but the rabbis explain that this law was applicable only inside the Holy Land prior to the law-giving at Sinai, and Jacob at the time of his marriages was outside of Israel's boundaries.

Commandment 31

One may not have sex with a menstruating woman or one that has not gone to mikvah at the appropriate time [Lev. 18:19]. Commandment 11 refers to noncarnal contact.

Commandment 32

"You shall not lie with a man as with a woman, it is an abhorrence" [Lev. 18:22].

Commandment 33

"Do not have carnal relations with any beast and defile yourselves thereby" [Lev. 18:23]. Directed to men.

Commandment 34

"Let no woman lend herself to a beast to mate with it; it is a perversion" [Lev. 18:23]. As is clear until now, most of these laws are directed to men. This is one of the few explicitly directed to women.

Commandment 35

A Kohen priest may not marry a woman who is or has been a prostitute [Lev. 21:7] [Yevumos 53–79].

Commandment 36

A Kohen may not marry a divorced woman [Lev. 21:7]. This law is increasingly being circumvented by creative annulments of the divorcée's first marriage.

Commandment 37

A Kohen must only marry a virgin [Lev. 21:13].

Commandment 38

A Kohen Gadol [high priest] may not marry a widow [Lev. 21:14].

Commandment 39

A Kohen Gadol may not have sex with those forbidden to him, even outside marriage [Lev. 21:15] [Yevumos 59].

Commandment 40

It is forbidden to castrate or sterilize any human or animal [Lev. 22:24] [Shabbos 111; Bava Metzia 90].

Commandment 41

On Yom Kippur you shall "afflict your souls," including an abstinence from sexual relations [Lev. 23:27].

Commandment 42

A cure for a man's jealousy: A woman suspected of being unfaithful by her husband, and twice warned by her husband in front of two witnesses, who is thereafter seen by two witnesses as entering into a secluded space with the man accused of being her adulterer, may be summoned by her husband to the Kohen priest. She could be cleared by drinking a mystical potion [this is unknown in modern times]. If innocent, the potion would have no effect. If guilty, she would die. If innocent, she will be blessed to conceive, as reparations for the false accusation and as a symbol of her sexual reconciliation with her husband. There is no scriptural equivalent for dealing with a woman's jealousy of a straying husband [Num. 5:11–31] [Sotah].

Commandment 43

The tzitzit tassels "shall be your fringe; look at it and recall all the commandments of the Lord and observe them, so that you do not follow your heart and your lustful urge" [Num. 15:38–39]. This is often interpreted to include a prohibition against pornography and other sins that are stirred by visual arousal or emotion rather than action [Brachos 12].

Commandment 44

"You shall not intermarry with them: do not give your daughters to their sons or take their daughters for your sons" [Deut. 7:3] [Yevumos 23; Sanhedrin 82]. However, if a woman marries a non-Jew her children are considered completely Jewish for all rabbinic legal and spiritual purposes. Additionally, if the non-Jewish partner converts to Judaism, it is not considered an intermarriage.

Commandment 45

A king "shall not have many wives, lest his heart go astray; nor shall he amass silver and gold to excess" [Deut. 17:17]. Even when something is allowed, or is a privilege of societal position, there is a prohibition against excess.

Commandment 46

Before a battle, the High Priest must speak to the people, saying, among other things, that a soldier who is engaged to be married is excused from battle [Deut. 20:2–7] [Sotah 42]: "Is there anyone who has built a new house but has not dedicated it? Let him go back to his home, lest he die in battle and another dedicate it. Is there anyone who has planted a vineyard but has not harvested it? [Psalm 128 compares the mother of children, or a pregnant woman, to a fruitful vine.] Let him go back to his home lest he die in battle and another harvest it. Is there anyone who has paid a bride-price for a wife but who has not yet married her? Let him go back to his home, lest he die in battle and another marry her" [Sotah 42].

Commandment 47

"And if [in wartime] you see among the captives a beautiful woman" [Deut. 21:11–14], one must comply with a set of laws protecting her rights [Yevumos 47; Kiddushin 81]. She is allowed a month to mourn her losses and family before she may be taken as a wife.

Commandment 48

If the aforementioned "beautiful captive" is no longer desired, she must be released outright and not sold for money or enslaved [Deut. 21:14].

Commandment 49

"A woman must not put on a man's apparel" [Deut. 22:5].

Commandment 50

". . . nor shall a man wear women's clothing, for whoever does these things is abhorrent to the Lord your God" [Deut. 22:5] [Nazir 59].

Commandment 51

"A man marries a woman and cohabits with her." Interpreted as meaning that a man must marry a woman in accordance with Biblical laws [Deut. 22:13] [Kiddushin].

Commandment 52

If a man falsely accuses his wife of not being a virgin when she wed, he is to be flogged, fined, and forbidden to leave or divorce her [Deut. 22:13–21] [Sanhedrin 8; Ketubot 44].

Commandment 53

Rape is a capital crime, and it is forbidden in any way to punish a woman who is forced to have sex against her will. "But if a man comes upon an engaged girl in the open country, and the man lies with her by force, only the man who lay with her shall die. But you shall do nothing to the young girl" [Deut. 22:25–26] [Baba Kamma 28; Avodah Zara 54; Ketubot 51].

Commandment 54

"If a man comes upon a virgin who is not engaged and he seizes her and lies with her, and they are discovered, the man who lay with her shall pay the girl's father 50 [shekels] of silver, and she shall be his wife. Because he violated her, he shall never have the right to divorce her." She, however, has that right. The keys to this commandment are recognizing (1) that in certain societies a raped non-virgin would be considered unmarriageable; and (2) that the couple may be discovered, indiscretion being a major sin compounding the original abuse [Deut. 22:28–29].

Commandment 55

"No one whose testes are crushed or whose member is cut off shall be admitted into the congregation of the Lord." The premier Biblical commentator, Rashi, adds that one who cannot ejaculate sufficiently to impregnate, or who is infertile, may not marry [Deut. 23:2] [Yevumos 76].

Commandment 56

One who is born of a forbidden relationship, such as incest or adultery, is forbidden to marry a person in good standing, and is banned from God's assembly for ten generations [Deut. 23:3] [Yevumos 49, 78; Kiddushin 78].

Commandment 57

A Jewish woman is forbidden to marry a man from the nations of Moab or Ammon, even converts to Judaism. Men are allowed to marry Moabites or Ammonites, allowing Boaz to marry Ruth the Moabite [Deut. 23:4].

Commandment 58

It is forbidden for an Israelite male or female to serve as a cult prostitute [Deut. 23:18].

Commandment 59

It is forbidden to use money earned in prostitution for sacred purposes [Deut. 23:19] [Teruma 29, 30].

Commandment 60

Divorce is allowed provided the ritual procedures are adhered to [Deut. 24:3] [Gitten].

Commandment 61

A divorced man may not remarry his wife if she had been married in the interim period, even if she has been widowed or divorced [Deut. 24:4] [Yevumos 11].

Commandment 62

A newlywed is excused from military and other civic duties for one year. "He shall be exempt one year for the sake of his household, to give happiness to the woman he married" [Deut. 24:5].

Commandment 63

A childless widow must marry her husband's brother [Deut. 25:5–10] [Yevumos 13, 93]. If the brothers (in descending age order) of the deceased do not wish to marry the childless widow, they must perform a designated ceremony before a religious court, freeing the widow to marry whom she pleases [Deut. 25:9] [Yevumos 13–24, 101–106].

Commandment 64

"If two men get into a fight with each other, and the wife of one comes up to save her husband from his antagonist, and puts out her hand and seizes him by his genitals, you shall cut off her hand. Show no pity" [Deut. 25:11–12].

Commandment 65

To "walk in [God's] way" [Deut. 28:9]. While this may not seem overtly sexual, this is the "way" to a successful relationship. The Torah [Exodus 34:6] describes God as "compassionate and gracious, slow to anger, abounding in kindness and faithfulness." Surely, a lover should do no less.

Appendix Two

A Biblical Glossary

What follows is a selected reference to topics revealing the range and spirit of Biblical opinion and values pertaining to sexuality and romantic relationships.

Adultery

"For the land is full of adulterers" [Jer. 23:10].

"An adulteress will prey upon a precious life. Can a man take fire to his bosom and not be burned? Can one walk on hot coals and not be seared? So is he who goes in to his neighbor's wife. Whoever touches her shall not be innocent" [Prov. 6:26–29].

"Whoever commits adultery is devoid of sense; only one who would destroy himself does such a thing" [Prov. 6:32].

"The eyes of the adulterer watch for twilight, thinking 'No one will glimpse me then.' He masks his face. In the dark they break into houses" [Job 24:15].

Anarchy

Widespread tribal immorality, gang rape, homosexual mobs, societal chaos, and civil war. Israelites would not marry anyone from the tribe of Benjamin, considered the most perverse group. "In those days, when there was no king in Israel, everyone did what was right in his own eyes" [Jud. 19–21].

Bad to the Bone

"Behold, I was born with iniquity, with sin my mother conceived me" [Ps. 51:7].

Beauty

"The sons of God saw the daughters of men, that they were beautiful; they took wives from among those that pleased them" [Gen. 6:2].

Before entering Egypt, Abraham tells Sarah, "I know what a beautiful woman you are. If the Egyptians see you and think, 'She is his wife,' they will kill me and let you live." Egyptians and Pharaoh are indeed attracted to her [Gen. 12:11–20].

Rebecca "was very beautiful to behold, a virgin whom no man had known" [Gen. 24:16].

"Leah's eyes were delicate, but Rachel was shapely and beautiful" [Gen. 29:17].

Abigail [David's wife] "was a woman of intelligence and beautiful appearance" [1Sam. 25:3].

From the roof, King David saw a woman bathing; she was "very beautiful to behold. The king sent someone to make inquiries about the woman" [2Sam. 11:2–5].

David's beautiful daughter, Tamar. Her step-brother Amnon "became infatuated with her" [2Sam. 13:1].

"Now in all of Israel there was no one who was praised as

much as Absalom for his good looks; from the sole of his foot to the crown of his head, he was without blemish" [2Sam. 14:25].

"You make his beauty melt away like a moth" [Ps. 39:12].

"Let the king be aroused by your beauty because he is your lord, worship him" [Ps. 45:11].

"The glory of young men is their strength; the splendor of old men is their gray hair" [Prov. 20:29].

"Charm is deceitful and beauty is vain, but a woman who fears God shall be praised" [Prov. 31:30].

King orders Vashti "to show her beauty to the people" [Est. 1:11].

Esther "was lovely and beautiful" [Est. 2:7].

"Let beautiful young maidens be brought before the king" [Est. 2:2].

"In all the land there were no women as beautiful as the daughters of Job" [Job 42:15].

Bedroom

"Elisha, the prophet in Israel, tells the king of Israel the very words that you speak in your bedroom" [2Kin. 6:12].

"Let the pious be joyful in glory; let them sing aloud upon their beds" [Ps. 149:5].

"I have spread my bed with tapestry, colored coverings of Egyptian linen. I have perfumed my bed with myrrh, aloes, and cinnamon" [Prov. 7:16–17].

"By night on my bed I sought the one I love; I sought him but I did not find him" [Song 3:1].

"My beloved has gone down to his garden, to the bed of spices, to feed his flock in the gardens, to gather lilies. I am my beloved's and my beloved is mine" [Song 6:2, 3].

Body

"I am awesomely, wondrously made, marvelous are your works, and that is something my soul knows very well" [Ps. 139:14].

Breasts

"I let you grow like the plants of the field; growing till womanhood, until your breasts became firm and your hair sprouted. You were still naked and bare when I passed by you and saw that your time for love had arrived. So I spread My robe over you and covered your nakedness, and I entered into a covenant with you by oath," declares the Lord God [Ezek. 16:7].

"Thus you reverted to the wantonness of your youth, remembering your youthful breasts, when the men of Egypt handled your nipples" [Ezek. 23:21].

"Let your fountain be blessed and rejoice with the wife of your youth. As a loving deer and a graceful doe, let her breasts satisfy you at all times. And always be enraptured with her love" [Prov. 5:18–19].

"A bundle of myrrh is my beloved to me, that lies all night between my breasts. My beloved to me is like a cluster of henna blooms, in the vineyards of Ein Gedi" [Song 1:13–14].

Bride

Arrangements for Rebecca to marry Isaac, her family's blessing, and "Isaac brought her into his mother's tent, and he took Rebecca and she became his wife, and he loved her" [Gen. 24:1–67].

"I will greatly rejoice in the Lord; my soul shall be joyful in my God, for He has clothed me with the garments of salvation. He has covered me with the robe of righteousness, as a bridegroom decks himself with a garland, as a bride adorns herself with her jewels" [Is. 61:10].

"As the bridegroom rejoices over the bride, so shall your God rejoice over you" [Is. 62:5].

Ruth and Boaz [Ruth 4:10–15].

Chastity

Joseph refuses the sexual offers of Potiphar's wife [Gen. 39:7–21].

"Do not lust after her beauty in your heart" [Prov. 6:25].

"I have made a covenant with my eyes; why then should I look upon a young woman?" [Job 31:1].

"If my heart has been enticed by a woman, or if I have lurked at my neighbor's door, then let my wife grind for another, and let others kneel over her" [Job 31:9–12].

Concubine

Abraham with Hagar [Gen. 16].

Nahor with Reumah [Gen. 22:24].

Jacob with Bilha and with Zilpa [Gen. 30:3–13].

Eliphaz with Timna [Gen. 36:12].

A beautiful woman captive [Deut. 21:10–14].

Gideon with woman of Shechem [Jud. 8:31].

Concubine raped by mob [Jud. 19:1–30].

Saul and Rizpeh [2Sam. 3:7].

David, "many wives and concubines in Jerusalem" [2Sam. 5:13].

Solomon "loved many foreign women in addition to Pharaoh's daughter . . . from which the Lord has said to the Israelites, 'None of you shall join them and none of them shall join you' " [1 Kin. 11:1].

Belshazzar and concubines drink from Temple vessels [Dan. 5:2].

Caleb and Ephah [1 Chr. 2:46].

Manasseh and Aramean woman [1 Chr. 7:14].

Rehoboam had eighteen wives and sixty concubines [2 Chr. 11:21].

Condemnation

"When he heard all that his sons were doing to all Israel, and how they lay with the women who performed tasks at the entrance to the [holy] Tent of Meeting, he said to them, 'Why do you do such things? I get evil reports about you' " [1 Sam. 2:22].

David condemned for murder of Uriah and adultery with Batsheva [2 Sam. 12:1–25].

Contentious Women

Esau, aged 40, takes two wives "and they were grief of mind to Isaac and Rebecca" [Gen. 26:34–35].

Samson fell in love with Delilah. The lords of the Philistines went up to her and said, "Coax him and find out what makes him so strong, and how we can overpower him, tie him up, and make him helpless; we'll each give you 1,100 shekels of silver." She said to Samson, "How can you say you love me when you won't confide in me?" [Jud. 16:4–31].

"It is better to dwell in a corner of an attic than in a roomy house with a brawling woman" [Prov. 21:9].

"It is better to dwell in the wilderness than with a contentious and shrewish woman" [Prov. 21:19].

"A continual dripping on a rainy day and a contentious woman are alike. As soon repress her as repress the wind, or grab oil with your right hand" [Prov. 27:15].

Corruption

God prepares for the Great Flood after seeing "all flesh had corrupted their way on earth" [Gen. 6:11–12].

Courtship

Hagar finds an Egyptian wife for Ishmael, while he was living in the wilderness [Gen. 21:21].

Abraham arranges Isaac's marriage [Gen. 24:1–67].

Without matchmaker, Jacob falls in love with Rachel, kisses her before meeting her parents. "Jacob served seven years for Rachel, and they seemed like just a few days to him because of the love he had for her." Rachel's father says, "It must not be done in our country, to give the younger daughter before the elder daughter" [Gen. 29:1–30].

Samson, with his bare hands, kills a lion, impressing a Philistine woman whom he then marries [Jud. 14:1–20].

"Now Michal, Saul's daughter, loved David. And they told Saul, and the thing pleased him. So Saul said, 'I will give her to him, that she shall be a snare to him, and the Philistines may kill him' " [1Sam. 18:20–28].

Ruth goes in to where Boaz sleeps, lying next to him at midnight [Ruth 3:1–14].

"The king loved Esther more than all the other women" [Est. 2:17].

Dance

"As soon as you see the girls of Shiloh coming out to join in the dances, come out from the vineyards, let each of you seize a wife from among the girls of Shiloh" [Jud. 21:20].

"As the Ark of the Lord came into the City of David, Michal, Saul's daughter, looked through a window and saw King David leaping and whirling before the Lord, and she despised him in her heart." Michal told David, her husband, when he came home: "How glorious was the king of Israel today, uncovering himself in the eyes of the maids of his servants, as one of the base fellows shamelessly uncovers himself." Therefore, says the Bible, Michal "had no children to the day of her death" [2Sam. 6:16–23].

Discretion

A good man "will conduct and guide his affairs with discretion" [Ps. 112:5].

"As a ring of gold in a swine's snout, so is a beautiful woman who lacks discretion" [Prov. 11:22].

Emasculate

The illegality of emasculation [Deut. 23:2].

Delilah turns on Samson, "she weakened him and made

him helpless, his strength slipped away from him. . . . The Philistines seized him and gouged out his eyes" [Jud. 16:18].

Fertility

"Adam knew Eve his wife and she conceived" [Gen. 4:1].

God tells Abraham: Sarah will conceive [Gen. 17:17–21].

Angel tells Abraham: Sarah will conceive [Gen. 18:9–15].

Sarah conceives in old age [Gen. 21:2–8].

Isaac prays for Rebecca to conceive, and she does [Gen. 25:21].

Rachel begs Jacob, "Give me children, or I shall die." Jacob was incensed at Rachel, and said, "Can I take the place of God, who has denied you fruit of the womb?" [Gen. 30:1–2].

Rachel, barren, and Leah, who stopped conceiving, give Jacob their maidservants that he may have children with them. He has four more sons, two with each [Gen. 30:3–13].

God remembers Rachel, "opens her womb" [Gen. 30:22–24].

Angel's promise, and strict rules for the woman, leads to birth of Samson [Jud. 13:2–25].

Elkanah to his wife Hannah: "Why do you weep? Am I not better to you than ten sons?" She gives birth to Prophet Samuel [1Sam. 1:1–18].

Michal punished with infertility for mocking David's dancing before the Ark [2Sam. 6:16–23].

"She has no son and her husband is old," but she conceives [2Kin. 4:14–17].

"Your wife shall be like a fruitful vine, in the very heart of your house, your children like olive saplings around your table" [Ps. 128:3].

Fertility Herb (Mandrakes)

Reuben gives mandrake to his mother, Leah. Rachel asks Leah for some [Gen. 30:14–17].

"The mandrakes give off a fragrance, and at our gates are all manner of pleasant fruits, new and old, which I have laid up for you, my beloved" [Song 7:13].

Foreskin

Command of circumcision to Abraham [Gen. 17:10].

Abraham's son, Ishmael, servants, and household get circumcised [Gen. 17:23–27].

King Saul: "Then you shall say to David, 'The king does not desire any dowry but 100 foreskins from the Philistines, to take vengeance on the king's enemies' " [1Sam. 18:25].

"Circumcise yourselves to the Lord, remove the foreskins from your hearts" [Jer. 4:4].

Goddess Worship

"They forsook the Lord and served Baal and the Ashtarot" [Jud. 2:13].

Saul was murdered and "they placed his armor in the temples of Ashtarot [Astarte, pagan goddess associated with fertility] and they impaled his body on the wall of Bet-Shan" [1Sam. 31:10].

"Solomon followed Astarte the goddess of the Sidonians and Milcom the abomination of the Ammonites" [1Kin. 11:5,33].

Harlot

Tamar, with father-in-law [Gen. 38:13–27].

"The daughter of any priest, if she profanes herself by playing the harlot, she profanes her father. She shall be burned with fire" [Lev. 21:9].

Israelites whoring with Moabite women [Num. 25:1–9].

Rahab, madam [Josh. 2:1–22].

"Once Samson went to Gaza, met a whore and slept with her." His enemies waited to kill him at dawn, but he left the harlot at midnight [Jud. 16:1–3].

Jepthah's mother [Jud. 11:1–11].

"Rebel Israel has committed idolatry, I cast her off and handed her a bill of divorce; yet her sister, faithless Judah, was not afraid—she, too, went and whored. Indeed, the land was defiled by her casual immorality, as she committed adultery with the stones and trees" [Jer. 3:8].

"You have gone as a harlot after the nations, defiling yourself with their fetishes" [Ezek. 23:30].

The righteous turned rebellious are compared to one [Is. 1:21].

Hosea's wife [Hos. 1:3].

"Do not lust after her beauty, nor let her allure you with her eyes. For by means of a harlot, a man is reduced to his last crust of bread" [Prov. 6:24–25].

"For a harlot is a deep pit, an alien seductress is a narrow well. They lie in wait, as if for prey, and destroy the unfaithful among men" [Prov. 23:27–28].

"A companion of harlots wastes his wealth" [Prov. 29:3].

Gang Rape

Angels visit Lot in Sodom. A mob gathers outside his home: "Where are the men who came to you tonight? Bring them out to us that we may be intimate with them." Lot says, "I beg you, my friends, do not commit such a wrong. Look, I have two daughters who have not known a man. Let me bring them out to you, and you may do to them as you please, but do not do anything to these men, since they have come under the shelter of my roof." The mob yelled at Lot, "The fellow comes here as an alien and already he acts the ruler." They moved forward to break the door down, but the angels blinded them with light [Gen. 19:4–11].

"The men of the town, a depraved lot, had gathered around the house and were pounding on the door. They called to the aged owner of the house, 'Bring out the man who has come into your house, so that we may be intimate with him.' The owner of the house went out and said, 'Please, my friends, do not commit such a wrong. Since this man has entered my house, do not perpetrate this outrage. Look, here is my virgin daughter, and [my guest's] concubine. Let me bring them out to you. Have your pleasure of them, but don't do that outrageous thing to this man.' " The concubine was raped through the night and died [Jud. 19–21].

Husband

Adam, blaming Eve [Gen. 3:12].

"Your desire shall be for your husband, and he shall rule over you" [Gen. 3:16].

Isaac, loving Rebecca [Gen. 24:67].

Elkanah, sympathetic [1Sam. 1:8–23].

Nabal, rebel [1Sam. 25:2–42].

David, mocked [2Sam. 6:20].

Ahab, sullen [1Kin. 21:5–16].

God, "For your Maker is your husband" [Is. 54:5].

"Her husband is known at the city gates, he sits among the elders of the land" [Prov. 31:23].

Job's wife was frustrated, saying, "You still keep your integrity! Curse God and die" [Job 2:9].

Incest

Lot's daughters seduce their father [Gen. 19:30–35].

"Reuben went and lay with Bilhah, his father's concubine" [Gen. 35:22].

Absalom hated Amnon because he had violated his sister Tamar [2Sam. 13:1–39].

Jealousy

Abraham fears the magnetism of Sarah's beauty on Egyptian men [Gen. 12:12].

Sarah sees Ishmael, the son of Abraham's concubine Hagar, mocking Isaac. Sarah demands Abraham send Hagar and Ishmael from their home [Gen. 21:9–21].

"For jealousy is a husband's fury. He will show no pity on the day of vengeance. He will accept no ransom. He will refuse your bribe, however great" [Prov. 6:34–35].

"For love is as strong as death, jealousy as cruel as the grave, its coals are the coals of fire, a most vehement flame" [Song 8:6].

Kissing

Jacob kisses Rachel before marriage [Gen. 29:11].

"Let him kiss me with the kisses of his mouth, for your love is better than wine" [Song 1:2].

Lewd Behavior

Cozbi and Zimri fornicating in public [Num. 25:1–18].

"So I took hold of my [murdered, raped] concubine, cut her in pieces, and sent her throughout all the territory of the inheritance of Israel, because they committed lewdness and outrage in Israel" [Jud. 20:6].

"[Even] the Philistine women are shocked by your lewd behavior" [Ezek. 16:27].

"I . . . will snatch away My wool and My linen, given to cover her nakedness. Now I will uncover her lewdness in the very sight of her lovers, and none shall save her from me" [Hos. 2:11].

Lovemaking

Isaac and Rebecca [Gen. 24:67].
   Jacob and Leah [Gen. 29:23, 30:16].
   Cozbi and Zimri [Num. 25:1–17].
   David and Batsheva [2Sam. 11:4].

Marriage

God creates Eve for Adam [Gen. 2:18–24].
   Jacob, Leah, and Rachel [Gen. 29:1–28].
   Caleb says, "He who attacks Kiryat Sepher and takes it,

to him I will give Achsah my daughter to be his wife" [Josh. 15:15–18].

"I remember you, the kindness of your youth, the love of your betrothal, when you followed me into the desert, into a land that was not sown" [Jer. 2:2].

"You shall not take a wife, nor shall you have sons or daughters in this place" [Jer. 16:2].

"The Lord has been witness between you and the wife of your youth, with whom you have broken faith, yet she is your companion and your wife by covenant" [Mal. 2:14].

"The royal princess, her clothing is woven with gold. She shall be led to the king in embroidered robes. The virgins, her companions, shall be presented to you. They are led in with joy and gladness, entering the palace of the king" [Ps. 45:13–15]

"Who is this coming out of the desert, like pillars of smoke, perfumed with myrrh and frankincense, with all the merchant's fragrant powders? It is Solomon's couch, with sixty valiant men around it" [Song 3:6].

Modesty, Lack of

A drunken, naked Noah is covered by his sons [Gen. 9:21–27].

"From the roof he saw a woman bathing" [2Sam. 11:2].

Nudity

"And they were both naked, the man and his wife and were not ashamed" [Gen. 2:25].

"Then the eyes of both of them were opened, and they knew that they were naked, and they sewed fig leaves together and made themselves coverings." God then asks, "Who told you that you were naked?" [Gen. 3:7–11].

Michal to her husband David: "How glorious was the king of Israel today, uncovering himself today in the eyes of the maids of his servants, as one of the base fellows shamelessly uncovers himself" [2Sam. 6:20].

"When I passed by you again, and looked upon you, indeed your time was the time of love. So I spread My wing over you and covered your nakedness. Yes, I swore an oath to you and entered into a covenant with you" [Ezek. 16:8].

Perfume

"You went to the king with ointment, you have provided many perfumes" [Is. 57:9].

"I have perfumed my bed with myrrh, aloes, and cinnamon" [Prov. 7:17].

"Ointment and incense delight the heart" [Prov. 27:9].

Pleasure from Sex

Having been promised a child, "Sarah laughed within herself, saying, 'After I have grown old, shall I have pleasure, [Abraham] being old also?' " [Gen. 18:12].

"Whatever my eyes desired, I did not keep from them. I did not restrain my heart from any pleasure . . . indeed all was vanity, grasping after wind" [Eccl. 2:10, 11].

Polygamy

After killing a man, Lamech runs to his two wives [Gen. 4:19–24].

"If a man has two wives, one loved and the other unloved" [Deut. 21:15–17].

"Gideon had seventy sons who were his own offspring, for he had many wives" [Jud. 8:30].

Elkanah had two wives; Peninah had children, Hannah did not [1Sam. 1:2].

Solomon had "700 wives, princesses, and 300 concubines, and his wives turned away his heart . . . after other gods" [1Kin. 11:1–4].

Rehoboam sought many wives for his sons [2Chr. 11:23].

Rape

"And when Shechem . . . saw [Dina] he took her, and lay with her, and violated her." Her brothers go to war on her behalf, asking, "Should he treat our sister like a harlot?" [Gen. 34:1–31].

Amnon and Tamar [2Sam. 13:6–33].

Satan

The serpent tempts Eve [Gen. 3:1–7].

Satan tries to ensnare Job [Job 1, 2:10].

"Now Satan arose against Israel" [1Chr. 21:1].

Secrets

The wicked man says in his heart, "God has forgotten, He hides his face, He will never see it" [Ps. 10:11].

"A prudent man keeps his peace. A base fellow gives away secrets. But a trustworthy soul keeps a confidence" [Prov. 11:12–13].

"Do not disclose the secret to another, lest he who hears it expose your shame, and your reputation will be ruined" [Prov. 25:9].

Seduction

Serpent to Eve [Gen. 3:1–7].
    Shechem and Dina [Gen. 34:3–4].
    Potiphar's wife and Joseph [Gen. 39:1–21].
"Now King David was old and advanced in years, and they put covers on him but he could get no heat. Therefore his servants said to him, 'Let a young woman, a virgin, be sought for our lord the king, and let her stand before the king, and let her care for him, and let her lie in your bosom, that the lord our king may be warm.' So they sought for a lovely young woman throughout all the territory of Israel and found Avishag the Shunamite, and brought her to the king. And the young woman was very lovely, and she cared for the king and served him, but the king did not know her" [1Kin. 1:1–4].

Temptation

Tamar and Judah [Gen. 38:13–30].
    Potiphar's wife and Joseph [Gen. 39:1–21].
    Rahab and the Spies [Josh. 2:1].
    Delilah [Jud. 16:4–31].
    David and Batsheva [2Sam. 11:2–12:24].
    Jezebel the wicked queen [1Kin. 21:7].
"From the window of my house, through my lattice, I looked out and saw among the simple, noticed among the

youths, a lad devoid of sense. He was crossing the street near her corner, walking toward her house in the dusk of evening, and in the dark hours of night a woman comes toward him. Dressed like a harlot, with set purpose, she is bustling and restive. She is never at home. Now in the street, now in the square, she lurks at every corner. She lays hold of him and kisses him. . . . Brazenly she says, . . . 'I have decked my couch with covers of dyed Egyptian linen; I have sprinkled my bed with myrrh, aloe, and cinnamon. Let us drink our fill of love till morning; let us delight in amorous embrace. For the man of the house is away. He is off on distant journey. He took his bag of money with him and will return only at mid-month' " [Prov. 7:6–20].

Wedding Gifts

"The man took a golden nose ring weighing half-a-shekel, and two bracelets for her wrists weighing ten shekels" [Gen. 24:22].

"Then the servant brought out jewelry of silver and gold, and clothing, and gave them to Rebecca. He also gave precious things to her brother and mother" [Gen. 24:53].

Laban makes a wedding feast for Jacob and Leah [Gen. 29:22–30].

"Ask me ever so much dowry and gift, and I will give according to what you say to me, but give me the young woman as a wife" [Gen. 34:12].

"The daughter of Tyre will be there with a gift. The rich among the people will seek your favor" [Ps. 45:13].

Wife

"It is not good for man to be alone" [Gen. 2:18].

Lot's wife becomes pillar of salt [Gen. 19:26].

Michal despised David in her heart [2Sam. 6:15].

Jezebel and Ahab [1Kin. 21:1–29].

"A capable wife is the crown of her husband, but she who causes shame is like rot in his bones" [Prov. 12:4].

"He who finds a wife finds a good thing, and obtains favor from the Lord" [Prov. 18:22].

"She considers a field and buys it, from her profits she plants a vineyard. . . . She extends her hand to the poor, she reaches her hand to the needy. . . . Strength and honor are her clothing, she shall rejoice in the Days to Come. She opens her mouth with wisdom, on her tongue is the law of kindness. She watches over the ways of her household, and does not eat the bread of idleness. Her children rise up and call her blessed, her husband, too, and he praises her. Many daughters have done well, but you excel them all. . . . Give her the fruit of her hands, and let her own works praise her in the gates" [Prov. 31:16–31].

The king was furious with his wife Vashti's disobedience and has her disposed of, fearing that "the queen's behavior will make all wives despise their husbands" [Est. 1:17].

Job tells his wife, "You speak as one of the shameless women might talk. Should we accept only good from God and not accept evil? For all that, Job said nothing sinful" [Job 2:10].

Index